Copenhagen

D1380383

Copenhagen

Text by Norman Renouf
Updated by Marcus Brooke
Photography: Jon Davison
Cover photograph: Superstock/Steve Vidler
Layout: Media Content Marketing, Inc.
Cartography by Ortelius Design
Managing Editor: Tony Halliday

Fourth Edition 2002 (Updated 2004)

CONTACTING THE EDITORS
Every effort has been made to provide accurate information in this publication, but changes are inevitable. The publisher cannot be responsible for any resulting loss, inconvenience or injury. We would appreciate it if readers would call our attention to any errors or outdated information by contacting Berlitz Publishing, PO Box 7910, London SE1 1WE, England. Fax: (44) 20 7403 0290;
e-mail: berlitz@apaguide.co.uk; www.berlitzpublishing.com

100/306 REV

CONTENTS

● A (☞ in the text denotes a highly recommended sight

Copenhagen

THE CITY
AND ITS PEOPLE

Copenhagen (København in Danish), the capital of Denmark, is located on the eastern side of Zealand, the largest of Denmark's 406 islands, with only the Øresund (Sound) separating it from Sweden. It was founded by Bishop Absalon in 1167, and these days is home, including its greater metropolitan area, to about 1,500,000 of the country's estimated 5.2 million population. Incidentally, with a land area of just 43,000 sq km (16,630 sq miles), Denmark is the smallest yet most densely populated nation in northern Europe. The 291 people per square mile dwarfs the mere 46 per square mile in the neighbouring country of Sweden.

Connected by the south of Jutland to Germany, Denmark is the only Scandinavian country physically joined to the European mainland and, as such, it is the bridge between Scandinavia and the rest of the continent. Consequently, Denmark shares many of the characteristics of its Nordic neighbours: liberal welfare benefits coupled with a high standard of living, and a style of government that aims at consensus and the avoidance of petty bureaucracy. Yet Denmark is also more 'European' and accessible than the rest of Scandinavia, and its appeal is universal.

Copenhagen, with its strategic location at the mouth of the Baltic Sea, has become an important crossroads. In addition to offering air, sea, road and rail connections, it is a major seaport in its own right. The capital city is the political centre of Denmark, the seat of royalty – it has the oldest royal dynasty in Europe, now headed by Queen Margrethe II and her French-born husband, Prince Henrik – and also the cultural centre of the country. As such, it not only offers many historical

Liberal welfare benefits allow Danes to relax and enjoy their golden years.

elements, chief of which are the Christiansborg complex, Rosenborg Slot and the Amalienborg Palaces, a multitude of museums – more than 60 at the last count – and theatres. It has also claimed for itself a reputation as one of northern Europe's jazz capitals. Copenhagen is renowned for its shopping opportunities. Strøget — said to be the longest pedestrian street in the world — probably has the most eclectic array of stores to be found anywhere, and the nearby side streets and squares have an unquantifiable number of boutiques, antiques shops, glass and silver artists, and stores selling items for the home. Of course, most of these offer products by celebrated Danish – and Scandinavian – designers, combining functionality and aesthetics.

Copenhagen's attractions are much wider than just history, culture and shopping; one of its great appeals is the character of the Danes themselves. The people are gregarious, loquacious and, at one and the same time, charming and sarcastic. Besides all of this they simply love enjoying life, especially when it comes to the combination of family, friends, fine – and sometimes not so fine – food and, of course, copious amounts of drink. In fact, there is a word, almost unpronounceable in English, *hygge*, that loosely translated means a combination of warmth, well-being and intimacy. This can be felt at all times in every part of Copenhagen, but is more obvious, especially on public holidays and warm sunny days, in the many parks, such as Rosenborg Have and Ørstedsparken, and popular meeting places like Rådhuspladsen and Nyhavn that make this such an attractive city. Nowhere is it more evident than in that world-famous Danish institution and crown jewel of the city, Tivoli Gardens.

A strong sense of fantasy and colour fills the atmosphere in Copenhagen. Postmen wear bright red jackets and ride yellow bicycles, chimney-sweeps pass by wearing black top hats and buses drive along with red and white Danish flags fluttering on both sides of the cab.

Although Copenhagen is a major capital city, it is very compact, with a well-preserved old-town area of winding cobbled streets, stuccoed houses and a network of canals, and most everything is easily accessible by foot. Despite the fact that the public transport system is superb, walking around Copenhagen is, in reality, the best way to discover this city's inestimable charms.

Long before the phrase was immortalised in song by Danny Kaye, Copenhagen was known to be 'wonderful, wonderful' – a clean, green city full of gaiety, culture and charm, with a tradition of tolerance and humour.

But that's not all. Within a very short distance of Copenhagen, and easily accessible on daytrips, are three major places of interest: Roskilde with its superb cathedral and Viking Ship Museum; Hillerød's beautiful Frederiksborg Castle; and Helsingør's dramatic Kronborg Castle used by Shakespeare in his great drama, *Hamlet*. Beyond these, Sweden lies just across the Øresund. There are two principle destinations across the water: Helsingborg and Malmø. Helsingborg is directly opposite Helsingør, and is reached in less than half an hour on one of the numerous ferries that ply the sound. Malmø, much larger and sharing with Copenhagen Kastrup International Airport, can be reached by road or rail over the Øresund Bridge, opened in 2000, in 35 minutes.

Other destinations worthy of consideration are Dragør, a small fishing village near the airport where an unusual number of the shops are open on Sunday in summer, the fashionable suburb of Klampenborg with its pleasant beach, wild deer park and Arne Jacobsen's Bellavista housing development and Bellevue Theatre, and the Louisiana Museum of Modern Art at Humlebæk, in a sublime setting on the coast north of Copenhagen.

Copenhagen is a place of many colours and surprises. Here, an aerial view of the magnificent city.

A BRIEF HISTORY

Well before the Vikings organised themselves into an extraordinary nation of seafarers, Denmark was inhabited by hunting peoples. Prehistoric relics of all kinds – some dating back to 50,000 BC – are displayed in Copenhagen's museums. The oldest surviving costumes in Europe have been found in this area, as have various musical instruments, including more than 30 examples of the Danish lur, which emits hoarse notes that seem strangely out of keeping with the long, graceful S-shaped stem characteristic of the instrument.

Viking Age

The first written records of the Vikings appear around AD 800, at which time Viking raids on neighbouring European countries were becoming notorious. At their peak, these fearless warriors had reached Newfoundland, were rounding the North Cape, and were making sallies to England, Holland, France, Spain, the Mediterranean and even as far east as the Caspian Sea. Prime examples of their boats are on display at the Roskilde Viking Ship Museum *(see page 76)*.

Danish raids upon England gathered in strength during the late 10th century and the first years of the 11th century, culminating in an attempt at conquest. Canute (Knud) the Great, after meeting considerable resistance, finally became king of England in 1016. The union was to last until 1042.

Christianity had been introduced into Denmark in 826 by a Benedictine monk, and received the royal seal of approval in 961 when King Harald (Blue-tooth) was converted by a monk named Poppo, who convinced him by seizing red-hot irons in his bare hands. A large runic stone set up by Harald at Jelling in East Jutland records that he had 'won for himself all Denmark

and Norway and made the Danes Christians'.

Medieval Times

In 1157, Valdemar I (the Great), came to the throne. He leaned heavily on the influence of Bishop Absalon of Roskilde, and this proved a partnership of critical importance to Copenhagen, then just a little fishing village called Havn. With its fine harbour on the Sound (Øresund in Danish) – the waterway between Denmark and Sweden, which forms the main entrance to the Baltic – the village found itself well-placed on what was becoming one of the main trading routes of medieval Europe. War-hero as well as statesman, Bishop Absalon forti-

Ancient Viking graves at Lindholmhoeje, on the Jutland peninsula.

fied Havn by constructing a castle on its small harbour island of Slotsholmen in 1167; this is now acknowledged to be the founding date of the modern city.

The name Havn became Køpmannæhafn ('merchants' harbour') in 1170, and eventually København. Today, Slotsholmen lies at the heart of the city. The impressive Christiansborg parliament buildings now occupy the site, but you can see some intriguing remnants of Absalon's castle in their cellars *(see page 34)*.

In the 12th century Denmark sorely overextended itself in all directions, and for this it paid dearly in the 13th and 14th centuries. It had interfered in the government of Schleswig and Holstein as well as troubling the growing trade of the North German Hanseatic ports. The Germans marched into Jutland. The Danish aristocracy seized the opportunity to curb the powers of its monarchy, and in 1282 King Erik V was forced to sign a Great Charter under which he would rule together with the nobles in the Council of the Danish Realm (Danmarks Riges Råd).

Nevertheless, Valdemar IV Atterdag (c.1320–75), probably the greatest of medieval Danish kings, led the country back onto a path of conquests and into new conflict with its Nordic neighbours, setting a pattern that was to last, intermittently, for centuries.

Denmark's hand was greatly strengthened when Valdemar's daughter, Margrete, married Håkon VI, King of Norway and Sweden. After his death, Margrete succeeded through the Treaty of Kalmar in 1397 in unifying the three Nordic powers under her nephew Erik VII of Pomerania. Indomitable Margrete ruled in his name, but was struck down by the plague at the peak of her power in 1412.

Holger the Dane

The Viking warrior Holger lived in the early 9th century. He travelled abroad and came back to Denmark in a time of trouble to help fight the country's enemies. Legend has it that he never died, but just went to sleep, waking whenever Denmark was threatened. During World War II, a section of the Resistance adopted the name of Holger Danske. There is a statue of Holger in Kronborg Castle at Helsingør (see page 70).

Egeskov Castle, a fortified manor on the island of Funen, was built in 1554, during the Reformation.

During the later, true reign of Erik VII (1412–39), Copenhagen was enlarged. The city then became the official Danish capital under Christopher III of Bavaria in the 1440s; when a university was founded by Christian I in 1479, it also became the country's cultural centre. By this time, the city's population had increased to about 10,000; Schleswig-Holstein was again under Danish rule, and a castle was being built at Helsingør (the Elsinore of Shakespeare's *Hamlet*) to enforce the payment of tolls on the Øresund. Control of the Øresund was vital to Denmark's strategic strength at the crossroads of the northern seas. Dues were exacted from each ship passing through the 3-km (2.5-mile) wide channel between Helsingør on Zealand and Helsingborg in Sweden.

By then Denmark stood in a very strong position. Forests had been cleared; new towns and villages had mushroomed. The scene was set for a turbulent period of 200 years marked by civil war against the nobles, the advent of the Lutheran movement in Denmark, and more wars with Sweden. In 1523 the Swedes revolted after the infamous 'Stockholm Bloodbath', causing the dissolution of the Kalmar Union and the independence of Sweden, although Denmark and Norway remained united.

The Reformation

In the 16th century, with the unprecedented spread of ideas, the latent, deep-seated discontent regarding abuses within the Catholic Church began to be brought out into the open. In Denmark, Catholic bishops had long been putting their wealth to political and military uses, and it was left to Christian III (1534–59), to break their stranglehold. He declared himself supreme authority of a state church based on Lutheranism in 1536, which had made deep inroads since arriving from Germany. The bishops were imprisoned until they 'consented', their wealth commandeered to pay royal debts and train new pastors.

Meanwhile, the wars with Sweden lurched on disastrously, with fortunes turning in the favour of the Danes' enemies. By the latter half of the 17th century Denmark had been forced to relinquish her remaining Swedish possessions, and to cede the east bank of the Øresund to Sweden. This crucial waterway was now split down the middle, jointly controlled by the two Scandinavian powers, as it still is today.

As Denmark licked its many 17th-century war wounds, the city of Copenhagen was given two great consolations. It was declared a free city in 1660 as an acknowledgement of its bravery during a two-year blockade by Sweden, and this meant that all residents were accorded the same privileges as the nobles. Second, under Christian IV it had experienced a wave of new culture and fine building. The 'Great Builder', as he was known, had effectively doubled the size of the city during the earlier part of the century. He was responsible for the existence of so many of the monumental green copper roofs that make the Copenhagen skyline uniquely photogenic, most notably among them the Round Tower, the Stock Exchange and the magnificent Rosenborg Castle.

Absolute Power

As a result of the Swedish wars, Denmark was bankrupted and its country laid-waste, and both political and social upheavals became inevitable.

In 1660, King Frederik III matched the mood of the moment and proclaimed himself absolute monarch, thereby depriving all the nobles of the Council of the Danish Realm of the powers they had enjoyed almost without a break since 1282. However, Frederik's absolute rule presided over a period of national unity, with a tightly controlled, well-organised central bureaucracy.

The early absolutist kings still waged several costly wars, mainly against the Swedish. Copenhagen suffered a terrible plague in 1711–12 which killed off 22,000 people – nearly a third of its inhabitants – as well as two devastating fires in 1728 and 1795 that necessitated major reconstruction of much of the city.

The 18th century was highlighted by major social advancements. Serfdom was abolished in 1788 (note the Freedom Pillar in Vesterbrogade, opposite the Central Station) and peasants threw off the yoke of the medieval landlord and began to work for themselves.

They began to move away from the central farmhouse to construct their own dwellings and smallholdings in the surrounding fields. This self-emancipation gave the Danish countryside its present character of a landscape dotted with farms, and was of enormous influence in the shaping of modern Denmark.

Napoleon and the 19th Century

Denmark found itself reluctantly involved in the revolutionary wars of late-18th-century Europe. By maintaining their participation with Russia, Sweden and Prussia in the League of Armed Neutrality – intended to thwart Great Britain's claim to the right of searching all vessels at sea – Denmark brought down upon itself the ire of the British. In 1801, a fleet under admirals Nelson and Parker sailed into the bay of Copenhagen. During the ensuing battle, Nelson, so legend has it, raised a telescope to his blind eye so as to be able to deny having been aware of a signal to break off the engagement.

Afraid that Napoleon would take over the Dano-Norwegian fleet, Britain subsequently demanded its instant surrender. When the Danes refused to acquiesce, Copenhagen was blockaded and in 1807 subjected to a three-day bombardment by the British Navy. Denmark had no choice but to hand over what was left of its fleet to the British, only to be forced immediately afterwards to agree to an alliance with Napoleon, who was by then marching fast into Jutland.

When Napoleon was finally brought to his knees, Denmark emerged completely isolated on account of this alliance. Norway, already the home to a vigorous separatist movement, was handed over to Sweden in 1814 in payment of war debts, since Denmark's coffers had become empty. The formerly vast Danish territories overseas were reduced to Greenland, Iceland, the Faroes and the Virgin Islands.

Fifty years later Denmark was further reduced by the loss of the duchies of Schleswig and Holstein – a third of its home territory and two-fifths of its population – to Bismarck's Prussia. Following a spate of civil turmoil in Denmark provoked by the 1848 revolution in France, Frederik VII was forced to relinquish his absolute rule and hand over the reigns of power to the National Liberal Party.

A liberal constitution was drawn up with wide suffrage, and the Danish 'Golden Age' was all set to begin. Hans Christian Andersen (1805–75), the writer from Odense, was strolling the city streets, reading his fairy-tales to groups of admirers.

In the city, the old ramparts were demolished and new railways, factories and workers' housing blocks sprang up, so that by the late 19th century Copenhagen was a thriving industrial centre. In the last quarter of the century, social insurance programmes began to make an appearance – a bold and pioneering development.

Meanwhile, changes were beginning to take place in the countryside. The theologian and politician N.F.S. Grundtvig

The combined Danish and French fleet arrives, ready to fight, in a 19th-century painting by Carl Neumann.

(1783–1872), established his system of popular adult high schools in 1844 to improve the peasant's lot, and the first co-operative plans were afoot.

The 20th Century and Beyond

In 1901 an important landmark was reached in Danish constitutional history when a government based only on a majority in the lower chamber of parliament (Folketing) was appointed. The march of the common people brought them not only into the cities and urban areas, but also right into the political struggle. In 1915, the Liberal Democrats, Social Democrats and Radical Liberals jointly forced the abolition of electoral privileges in the upper chamber (Landstinget) and initiated a system of proportional representation for both chambers. At the same time, the vote was at last given to women and servants.

The new Danish society was put under severe strain in the process of adopting the compromises necessary to maintain neutrality during World War I. After the war North Schleswig voted itself back into Denmark, establishing the shape of today's border.

Industrial unrest and the severe economic depression between the two world wars failed to halt the progress of Denmark. In the design of consumer goods – furniture, cutlery, glass, pewter, silver and textiles – Denmark set new standards, combining utility with beauty, to the point where 'Danish design' became synonymous with good, functional, yet aesthetically pleasing articles.

When World War II broke out in 1939 the Scandinavian nations issued their declarations of neutrality but, nevertheless, on 9 April 1940 Denmark was invaded by Germany. Following a token struggle, the country's defences collapsed and the nation fell under German control. The Danish economy now found itself forced to adapt to the German market, and the country had no choice but to manifest a degree of compliance. However, the anti-Nazi sentiments of the vast majority of Danes were expressed by cold-shoulder treatment, and eventually acted upon through outright resistance. The Danes managed by various means to smuggle 7,000 of Denmark's 7,500 Jews out of the country and into neighbouring Sweden.

The wartime king, Christian X, became the country's folk-hero as he rode out every day among the crowds. In 1943, the government resigned – it could no longer yield to German demands without losing the support of the population – and the running of the country was left to heads of departments. Nevertheless, the resistance was so organised and so dominant that Denmark was already a full member of the Allied forces by the time the war came to an end in 1945.

So began a new era of massive Danish reconstruction, finally resulting in the present modern-day society – one of the world's most successful attempts at a welfare state – with a quality of life ranking among the highest in the world.

Politically, Denmark abandoned neutrality when it became a member of NATO in 1949. Economically, it was a founding member of the European Free Trade Association (EFTA), and joined the European Economic Community (subsequently the European Union) with the UK and Ireland in 1972. It also played a part in the revival of Nordic unity after the war, joining the Nordic Council and the Nordic Council of Ministers.

Denmark today is one of the most prosperous countries in Europe, and its population of 5 million enjoys an extremely high standard of living. Membership to the European exchange rate mechanism has ensured that its economy continues to grow in strength. The country made its biggest impact to date on the European Union in a 1992 referendum, when more than 50 percent of the population voted against the

A chamber of the Danish parliament; its members are elected by proportional representation.

Maastricht Treaty (which lays the foundation for European economic and political union). At the World Summit in Copenhagen in 1995, Denmark was one of the only countries to forgive a sizeable amount of Third-World debt. And the following year, it gained greater acclaim with the selection of Copenhagen as the 1996 'Cultural Capital of Europe'.

The fact that Denmark's influence is felt so far beyond its frontiers testifies to its important role in the future of a cohesive and integrated Europe. Notwithstanding this, in 2000 the people of Denmark again voted in a referendum that would affect their future; this time they voted not to adopt the Euro as a new currency.

In general elections held in 2001 the right-wing parties (Liberal and Conservative People's), on a platform of law and order, increased their popular vote to form a coalition government. The new prime minister, Anders Fogh Rasmussen, promised much stricter control of immigrants, although Denmark accepts fewer immigrants per capita than any other European country.

WHERE TO GO

Y ou will have no problem finding your way around this delightfully compact city. Most of the important sights are contained within the central section and bounded by the former medieval ramparts, so exploring Copenhagen on foot is a real pleasure. There is also the network of canals that offer many opportunities for waterside walks and gentle excursions afloat. And if you want a change of pace from sightseeing or shopping, the abundance of leafy parks and gardens provides a very welcome and pleasant retreat.

RÅDHUSPLADSEN

Every city has a social gathering point somewhere but surprisingly, Copenhagen has more than one. Without a doubt, the centrally located **Rådhuspladsen** (City Hall Square) is the most popular and, consequently, most of the suggested planned walks start from here. It is also the stopping point for the most important bus routes and is near Central Station, where trains depart for the suburbs and destinations outside of the city.

It is in this large open square, with a café and ubiquitous hot-dog stands *(pølsevogn)* – where tasty Danish sausages are served in a variety of inexpensive forms – that you can take the opportunity to observe Danish life.

The dominant building here is the red brick **Rådhuset** (City Hall) with its 105-m (345-ft) tower. Built between 1892 and 1905, it is reached via broad steps that play host to impromptu concerts. Its main doorway is crowned by a statue of Bishop Absalon, the founder of the city *(see page 12)*, in copper and 22-carat gilt. If you direct your view to the roof above you'll see six bronze figures of night watchmen dating from various periods of the city's

*Rådhusplasen, Copenhagen's City Hall Square,
is the centre and heart of the capital.*

history. Each section of Rådhuset bears a different style and
imprint, but they come together architecturally very much
like a patchwork quilt. The main hall and the banqueting
room are impressive with their statuary and coats-of-arms –
especially the view of the 44-m (145-ft) long hall from the
first-floor colonnade (guided tours Mon–Fri 3pm, Sat 10am
and 11am; tel: 33 66 25 82; <www. copenhagencity.dk>;
admission fee).

If you are feeling energetic, there are also guided tours of
City Hall Tower and its 300 steps (Jun–Sept Mon–Fri
10am, noon, 2pm, Sat noon, Oct–May Mon–Sat noon;
admission fee). On a clear day you can see across the
Øresund to Sweden and north along the coast to Elsinore. In
the foyer of City Hall you'll see the sign to **Jens Olsen's
World Clock** (open Mon–Fri 10am–4pm, Sat 10am–1pm;

The Lur Blowers Statue at Rådhusplasden stands watch over the bustling city centre.

admission fee). This most intriguing astronomical clock shows time around the world, the positions of the planets and the Gregorian calendar.

To your right as you leave the City Hall, on Vester Voldgade, is a statue that brings a smile to every Dane's face, the **Lur Blowers Statue**. Legend has it that the two men on top will sound a note on their instruments if a virgin passes by – although they've been standing on the column since 1914 they've led a life of silence. On the opposite corner of the square is the dramatic copper **Bull-and-Dragon Fountain** (1923), depicting a fierce, watery battle between the two beasts. Not far away sits a bronze version of Denmark's favourite son, storyteller Hans Christian Andersen, near the boulevard that bears his name. It is on this busy road that you'll notice a very prominent feature of Danish life – the ubiquitous bicycle. On the opposite side of Hans Christian Andersen Boulevard is one of the entrances to Copenhagen's most famous attraction: Tivoli Gardens *(see page 52)*.

The road to the northwest of Rådhuspladsen is Vesterbrogade, which leads to Central Station. The monument in the middle of this street is the Freedom Pillar that was erected between 1792 and 1797 to commemorate the end of serfdom for the Danish peasantry in 1788. It was designed by the artist Nikolaj Abildgård.

STRØGET AND THE OLD TOWN

If only because of its proximity to Rådhuspladsen, although there are many other reasons as well, the first place to visit after the square is Copenhagen's most famous – and the world's longest – pedestrian-only street. Known as, although not officially named, Strøget (pronounced stroy-et) this is actually a continuation of four streets: Frederiks-berggade – leading off Rådhuspladsen – Nygade Vimmel-skaftet, Amergertorv and Østergade, that wind their way for 1 km (about ¾ mile) to Kongens Nytorv square. Day or night, this traffic-free haven is never boring and offers visitors an amazingly eclectic array of shops – from the tacky tourist variety to upmarket, expensive speciality stores – along with numerous small bars, restaurants, cafés and an abundance of street performers. Don't be afraid to wander off Strøget to explore the small streets around it. Each of these in turn has its own surprises

Danish storyteller Hans Christian Andersen is immortalised in bronze.

among the numerous antiques shops, speciality stores and boutiques as well as fashionable restaurants.

That said, it must also be stated that the entrance to Frederiksberggade, dominated as it is by fast-food outlets, is not exactly prepossessing; however, perseverance will bring its rewards. Where Frederiksberggade ends, Strøget opens out into two squares on either side of the street. **Gammeltorv**, to the left, is a popular place for small market stalls and is home to the **Caritas Fountain** which, dating from 1610, is the city's oldest. In a tradition going back to the golden wedding of King Christian IX and Queen Louise in 1892, imitation golden apples are made to dance on the jets of the fountain on the monarch's birthday (now 16 April). **Nytorv**, on the other side, is dominated by the impressive architecture of the law courts. Each of these

Strøget changes names four times along its length, but it always remains traffic-free.

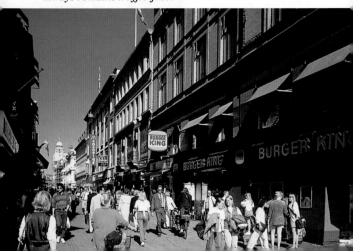

squares is a good place to sit at a street café and watch the procession of passing people.

The next place of note is the **Helligåndskirke** (Church of the Holy Ghost). Built in the 17th–18th century, it is set in its own small gardens. Outside is an area particularly popular with street performers and other hawkers. Just past this point, Strøget opens out again and on the left side of Amagertorv you'll see a fine example of Dutch Baroque buildings — home to the group of **Royal Copenhagen** shops *(see page 82)*. One of these, at No 6, is the Royal Copenhagen Porcelain store, an Aladdin's cave with an elegant restaurant and small museum. It dates from 1616. Across the road is W.Ø. Larsen, dating from 1864, a tobacconist in whose basement is a small, but interesting **Tobacco Museum** (open Mon–Thurs 10am–6pm, Fri 10am–7pm, Sat 10am–5pm; free).

A few steps further, at the junction of Amagertorv and Østergade, another busy pedestrian-only street, Købmagergade, leads off to the left. At No 24 is the **Museum Erotica** (open May–Sept daily 10am–11pm; Oct–Apr Sun–Fri 11am–8pm, Sat 10am–10pm; admission fee). It claims to be the world's first serious erotic museum and was opened 25 years after pornography was legalised in Denmark in 1968.

Back on Strøget, now called Østergade, the shops are more upmarket and include the likes of Gianni Versace, Gucci, Hermès and Bang & Olufsen. Pause to look in the window of Halberstadt (No 4) – a jeweller founded in 1846 – which features a small train encrusted with gems that runs continually around.

AROUND KONGENS NYTORV

Kongens Nytorv, the 'King's New Square' of Christian V – dating from 1680 and still the city's largest (12 streets lead off it) – is surrounded by impressive stately buildings. The park in the centre of the square is dominated by the king himself, in the form of an elaborate equestrian statue of Christian V, with four classical figures seated submissively under his horse.

On the southwest side is **Det Kongelige Teater** (the Danish Royal Theatre; tel: 33 69 69 69; <www.kgl-teater.dk>), the country's most important cultural centre. Home of Danish national ballet, opera and drama, it was originally opened in 1748, rebuilt in 1874, and was briefly the stage of Hans Christian Andersen, who tried without success to become a ballet dancer.

Next to the theatre stands **Charlottenborg Slot**, the oldest building on the square. It was built as a royal palace in 1683 in the style of Dutch baroque and, since 1754, has

The Danish Royal Theatre's stage was once the stomping ground of Hans Christian Andersen.

been the home of the Royal Academy of Fine Arts. Enter through the front gate and at the rear is **Charlottenborg Udstillingsbygning** (tel: 33 13 40 22; <www.charlottenborg-art.dk>), which exhibits Danish and international contemporary art (open daily 10am–5pm, Wed till 7pm; admission fee).

Look around the square and you will notice other splendid buildings. **Thotts Palae** (Thott's Mansion) in the northeast corner, was built for the naval hero Admiral Niels Juel and is now home to the French Embassy. Not to be outdone is the wonderful façade of the five-star **Hotel D'Angleterre**, arguably Denmark's finest hotel.

The unusually shaped building tucked between Store Strandstræde and Bredgage is the beautifully preserved 1782 **Kanneworffs Hus**, which houses Ravhuset, a shop selling jewellery made from Baltic amber; located above Ravhuset is a small **Amber Museum** (open daily May–Aug 10am–8pm, Sept–Apr 10am–6pm; tel: 33 11 67 00; admission fee). Diagonally across the square is the imposing **Magasin du Nord** with its impressive ornate façade. This was Scandinavia's first department store and is still its largest.

SOUTH OF STRØGET

Leave Kongens Nytorv by Vingårdsstraede at the southwest corner of Magasin du Nord. You'll find yourself in an area of jazz clubs, small bars and artists' hangouts. At its junction with Admiralgade is the massive 70-m (230-ft) tall copper spire of **Skt Nikolaj Kirke** (St Nicholas Church). Destroyed several times by fire and rebuilt as recently as 1917, it is no longer used for services but houses the **Copenhagen Contemporary Art Centre**, which has a small permanent collection and space for temporary exhibitions (open daily noon–5pm; tel. 33 19 16 26; <www.nikolaj-ccac.dk>; admission fee, Wed free).

At the south end of Admiralgade is **Holmens Kirke** (open Mon–Fri 9am–2pm, Sat 9am–noon; admission free). The church is in the Venetian style, but with Dutch gable ends and a small copper tower in the middle. The building was originally a 16th-century anchor forge but was transformed in 1619 by Christian IV into a sailors' church. On the altar, reredos and pulpit there is a profusion of oak carvings by Abel Schrøder the Younger. The church remains a favourite with the Royal Family; in 1967 Queen Margrethe was married here to Prince Henrik, formerly the French Count de Laborde de Montpezat. An adjoining chapel (built 1706–8) is dedicated to maritime heroes. Look for the model ship hanging from the ceiling, a tradition common in many Danish churches.

> Don't worry about trying to speak Danish; it's extremely difficult to pronounce, and everyone you'll meet will speak perfect English.

Outside Holmens Kirke you are now by the canal, and it is impossible not to be impressed by the Christiansborg complex on the opposite bank *(see page 32)*. Turn right up Ved Stranden and head for the Højbro bridge and the junction with Gammel Strand and Højbro Plads.

Within a short distance of here are three very different statues. The most obvious of these, on Højbro Plads, is the magnificent copper green statue of Bishop Absalon showing the warrior-priest in chain mail with axe in hand. On the corner of Gammel Strand stands the statue of the *Fiskerkone* (Fishwife), scarf on her head, shawl around her shoulders, wearing a stout apron and clasping a fish. Erected in 1940, she resembles the women who sit inside their stalls nearby every Tuesday–Friday morning, as fishwives have done here for centuries. The third sculpture is less obvious; in fact, you'll have to look over the bridge to discover the submerged depiction of the 'Mermaid with Seven Sons' that is attractively illuminated at night.

Next, turn into Gammel Strand itself; the name means 'old shore' and, as this implies, it is the former edge of the city. This is one of the two principal starting-points for canal boat tours, the other being in Nyhavn *(see page 39)*. Immediately across the canal lies a distinctive square-arched, yellow-ochre building with a classical-style frieze, looking like a national tomb. And that's really what it is – a monument to the great Danish sculptor Bertel Thorvaldsen (1770–1844) *(see page 35)*.

The humble pews of the sailors' Holmens Kirke serve as a comfortable refuge.

Off to the right, on Frederiksholms Kanal, you'll be able to make out the arched entrance to the colossal Nationalmuseet *(see page 36)*. Gammel Strand also has restaurants and bars, among which is the very elegant **Krogs**, the city's finest seafood restaurant.

Time now to proceed back to Rådhuspladsen, via a collection of interesting old streets. At the western end of Gammel Strand, Snaregade features some timber-framed houses. Continuing into into Magstræde and the houses at numbers 17 and 19 are two of the city's oldest, dating from 1640. Next is Vandkunsten, a delightful little square with outdoor cafés and a pretty fountain. The name of the square means 'water artifice' and it is here that Copenhagen's first water pipes were laid. Continue across the next junction into Gåsegade, and look for the gabled houses with 18th-century hoists at the top. Furniture is traditionally hauled up by these hoists, rather than being squeezed up the narrow stairwells.

On the corner of Hestemøllestræde and Lavendelstræde is a house where Mozart's widow lived with her second husband, a Danish diplomat. Here, the huge archways of Copenhagen's fourth town hall dominate; built between 1805 and 1815 it now houses the law courts. On Lavendelstræde you'll find typical Danish houses and shops from 1796, the year following the city's second great fire, and at the end of the street Vester Voldgade leads to Rådhuspladsen.

CHRISTIANSBORG, NATIONAL MUSEUM, NY CARLSBERG GLYPTOTEK MUSEUM

Starting at Rådhuspladsen, retrace your steps on the previous tour back to the Højbro bridge and then cross it to the small island of Slotsholmen and the imposing towers of Christiansborg. Stop a little further along the canal at the highly ornamented **Børsen** (Stock Exchange), dating from the days of Christian IV. Its green copper roof is topped by a spire composed of four twining dragon's tails. Christian IV was influenced by the booming Netherlands architecture of his day, and in 1619 commissioned two Dutch brothers to put up this somewhat quaint building. Currently it houses special events, and the Stock Exchange has since emigrated to Strøget.

Christiansborg is the sixth castle or palace to have stood here since Absalon built his fortress in 1167: pillage, fire and rebuilding frenzies have taken their toll on the earlier ones. The third castle became the permanent seat of the king and government in 1417. The present edifice dates from the early 20th century, at which time Thorvald Jørgensen won an

The exquisite marble bridge at Christiansborg.

architectural competition for the design of a new Christiansborg palace. On 15 November 1907, King Frederik VIII laid the cornerstone that had been hewn out of the granite remains from Absalon's original castle. Above this a vast plinth was made of 7,500 boulders donated by 750 Danish boroughs, and then the palace was faced with granite slabs. Look up to see 57 granite masks of Denmark's greatest men. Covered in copper between 1937 and 1939, the roof of Christiansborg makes an imposing addition to the city's verdigris skyline.

The chapel, theatre museum, riding stables and beautifully restored marble bridge that survived two disastrous fires in 1794 and 1884 help to give the palace a more venerable aspect than its more recent origins suggest. Today the castle houses government ministries, Parliament (*Folketing*) and the Danish Supreme Court, as well as being the centre of a complex of museums. The most notable highlights of the complex include the **Kongelige Repræsentationslokaler** (Royal Reception Chambers; guided tours in English: May–Sept daily 11am, 1pm and 3pm, Oct–Apr Tues, Thurs, Sat, Sun 3pm; tel: 33 92 64 92; admission fee).

This is a no-touch museum with strict rules, and is only open when the chambers are not being used for official receptions. In the entrance hall you will be provided with canvas slippers to put over your shoes, as you'll be walking on priceless parquet floors. One of the guide's first anecdotes will most probably be: 'Look at the roof here, held by pillars in the shape of male statues, heads bent to take the weight – a symbol of modern Danes paying their taxes…' Upstairs is a series of linked rooms, including the richly tapestried gold-and-green room where monarchs are proclaimed (Danish monarchs have not actually been crowned here since Christian VIII) from the balcony, which overlooks the Castle Square (Slotspladsen) below. The Great Hall is now home to *Les Gobelins*, a series of 11 tapestries commissioned by the Danish business community to mark the occasion of Queen Margrethe II's 50th birthday in 1990. These took so long to create that they were not dedicated until 12 April 2000, at which time the Queen donated them to the state.

In the palace basement you will find the extensive **Ruinerne af Absalons Borg** (Ruins of Absalon's Palace; open May–Sept daily 9.30am–3.30pm, Oct–Apr Tues, Thurs, Sat, Sun 9.30am–3.30pm; tel: 33 92 64 94 for tours; admission fee), from 1167, as well as remnants of more recent castles on the site. Also in the complex is the **Folketing** (Danish Parliament), and there are free tours (tel: 33 37 55 00; <www.slotte.dk>), although they have a rather limited schedule. Out in the vast parade ground and dominated by a copper equestrian statue of Christian IX, are the **Kongelige Stalde og Kareter** (Royal Stables; open May–Sept Fri, Sat–Sun 2pm–4pm, Oct–Apr Sat–Sun 2pm–4pm; admission fee). The stables are home to some fine driving and riding horses, which can sometimes be seen exercising in the square. On display are uniforms and royal carriages dating from 1778. Above the stables is the **Teatermuseet** (Theatre Museum; *see page 61*).

Thorvaldsens Museum, Porthusgade 2 (open Tues–Sun 10am–5pm, guided tours in English Jul–Aug 3pm; admission fee, Wed free), is located on the Gammel Strand side of the Christiansborg complex and is a museum of classical intent. The Roman and Greek gods and goddesses gazing down at you, however, are all 19th-century revivals of antiquity. They are the work of Bertel Thorvaldsen (1770–1844), the greatest of Danish sculptors.

Returning after 40 years in Rome – the Danish government fetched him back in triumph – Thorvaldsen devoted his library, collection and fortune to the creation of a museum of his own works, choosing a young architect, Gottlieb Bindesbøll, to design it. The result was one of Copenhagen's most distinctive, untypical buildings, with a decorated ochre façade, and interior walls and ceilings in black, reds, blues and oranges that contrast with the pure white plaster and marble of Thorvaldsen's sculptures.

Behind the Royal Stables, in side street, is yet another museum housed in a late 16th–early 17th-century building. The **Tøjhusmuseet** (Arsenal Museum; *for opening times, see page 62*) holds a fascinating collection of military items – from uniforms to planes – dating from the 15th century.

Close by are the **Library Gardens**; designed in 1920 these are a veritable oasis of peace and calm, and an ideal place to sit and rest. Although the building you see from the gardens only dates from 1906, Frederik III founded the **Danish Royal Library**, <www.kb.dk>, around 1653. In 1989 it was merged with the University Library, founded in 1482. Walk around the building to the waterfront and be prepared for a huge architectural surprise. On Søren Kierkegaards Plads a seven-storey, glass, granite, concrete and steel structure appears to be leaning towards the river. This, because of its colour, is affectionately known as the Black Diamond (completed in 1999), and is the annex for the Danish Royal Library. Concerts, lectures and meetings are also held here, and there are shops, restaurants and cafés.

On leaving the Black Diamond pause to look at the building currently being constructed across the water on the island of Dokøen. It is the massive new **Queen Margrethe Opera House**, which is scheduled to open in 2005. Now turn right then right again and follow the canal to Ny Vestergade and the **Nationalmuseet** (National Museum; *for opening times, see page 78)*. This is nothing less than a well-organised labyrinth of artefacts ranging from Stone-Age Danish rock carvings to Mongolian horse-riding equipment and tents. The biggest museum in Scandinavia, it consists of major collections, varying from prehistoric to modern Danish culture, Egyptian and classical antiquities, coins and medals, and ethnographical and children's displays.

Here you can study the prehistoric Denmark that led up to the extraordinary Viking times. Outstanding among Stone-Age exhibits is the Hindsgavle Dagger (1800–1500 BC), fashioned out of flint after bronze weapons in use elsewhere. The most striking exhibit is the Sun Chariot of 1200 BC. The Danes once worshipped the sun, imagining it just as it is

A vast repository of national culture is Nationalmuseet, where every inch is typical Danish design.

Ancient statues on display at Ny Carlsberg Glyptotek.

here: a disk of gold riding through the sky in a chariot behind a celestial horse.

Through its colonisation of Greenland, Danish culture opens doors onto Eskimo culture. The lively exhibition of huskies, igloos, reconstructed Eskimo camp and medieval clothes is worth a visit.

Before returning to Rådhuspladsen, cross to H.C. Andersen's Boulevard and head for the distinctive building just across from the Tivoli Gardens. This is home to **Ny Carlsberg Glyptotek** *(for opening times, see page 78)*. The Glyptotek was founded on the classical collection of Carl Jacobsen, a Danish brewer and art connoisseur (1842–1914), and was then developed by his family. Under its elaborate roof lies one of the world's foremost displays of Egyptian, Greek, Roman and Etruscan art, with enough statues and artefacts to equip 100 ancient temples. As the museum was specially built around the classical collection, you'll find unusual features such as the subtropical garden in the central hall, which appears to be transplanted directly from ancient Rome. In contrast the French collection – paintings by Gauguin, van Gogh and Monet, Rodin sculptures and a complete set of Degas bronzes, 73 delicate statues that won the painter posthumous acclaim as a sculptor – is housed in a glorious spacious new wing.

NYHAVN, AMALIENBORG AND THE LITTLE MERMAID

This walk begins at Kongens Nytorv (bus 26 from Rådhus-pladsen). Cross the square towards **Nyhavn**; the name literally means 'new harbour' and you'll immediately notice the nautical flavour of this one-time 'sailors' street'. Over the centuries the two sides of the canal have developed into a remarkable illustration of old Copenhagen. At the Kongens Nytorv end of the canal, which was dug in 1671 to enlarge the harbour, stands a sizeable old anchor, a memorial to the Danish sailors killed in World War II. On either side of the canal itself, an unusual collection of vessels lies at anchor with their masts colourfully bedecked with the Danish flag. This sight, combined with numerous restaurants and bars with outside terraces, and the antiques and other shops on the north side, draws thousands of people who are only too happy to eat, drink and socialise in such an attractive setting.

This is a street with everything – history, architecture, nightlife, a constant passage of colourful small vessels. It was even home to Hans Christian Andersen, who lived here first at number 67 from 1854–1864 and later at number 18.

Walk along Nyhavn on the north side, and you'll pass a superb hotel conversion of an 18th-century warehouse. Just beyond is a view over the inner harbour to the Christians-havn area where the spiralling steeple of Vor Frelsers Kirke dominates *(see page 55)*.

Turn left and walk along the waterfront and then bear left to Skt Annæ Plads, where you will most likely be met by the huge Oslo ferry tied up at the quayside (the terminal is due to close in 2005). This is a fine boulevard lined with consulates and distinguished old offices, but rather than follow it, turn right and walk along the waterfront to the pleasant

Stroll along Nyhavn to experience the buildings and boats of old Copenhagen and the restaurants and bars of today.

Amaliehavn Gardens. These were created by Belgian land-scape architect Jean Delogne in 1983 using French limestone and Danish granite. The bronze pillars around the fountain were designed by Italian sculptor Arnaldo Pomodoro.

The road leading away from the water takes you to one of the most attractively symmetrical squares in Europe, **Amalienborg Plads**. The huge equestrian statue of Frederik V, unveiled in 1771 and dominating the centre of the square, gives you a clue that you are now in the proximity of royal-ty. In fact, the four identical mansions (at least on their exte-rior) that line the octagonal perimeter of the square were originally constructed in 1749 as town mansions for four noblemen. However, after Christiansborg castle was destroyed by fire for the second time in 1794, the royal fam-ily slowly bought Amalienborg from the nobles, and has lived here since. Today, collectively known as **Amalienborg Palace**, these buildings are considered to be one of the finest Rococo ensembles in Europe.

Four roads converge at right angles on the courtyard, while bearskin-clad soldiers guard each of the palaces and corners, with an extra sentry posted at the gateway between the two palaces to your left. The queen lives in the right-hand wing next to the colonnade, the queen mother in the adjacent wing, and the two princes call the third home, which also houses the **Amalienborg Palace Museum** *(for opening times, see page 59)*. The fourth wing, directly to the left, is reserved as a guesthouse for state visitors. The name Amalienborg came from the wife of Frederik III, Queen Sophie Amalie.

The main Amalienborg attraction is the **changing of the Royal Life Guards**, whose principal duty is to guard the Queen at Amalienborg Palace. At 11.30am each day, the guards leave their barracks near Rosenborg Castle and march through the city's back streets so as to arrive in the palace

The changing of the guard at Amalienborg is a daily event that is rich with ceremony.

square just before noon, moving from one sentry-box to another in a series of foot-stamping ceremonies. Guardsmen march to the accompaniment of a full band when the Queen is in residence, their black bearskins rippling in the breeze. They also wear white-striped blue trousers and highly polished boots and, on festive occasions, red tunics with white shoulder straps.

Leave Amalienborg Plads via Amaliegade, to the road to the right, and follow it for about 730m (800yd) to its junction with Esplanaden where, across the road is Churchill Park, with several interesting sights.

The **Frihedsmuseet** (Danish Resistance Movement Museum, *see page 60*) is located on one of the prettiest spots in town – especially at daffodil time. Just past here, the British connection is continued in the form of **St Alban's Church**, (open May–Sept daily 10am–4pm), which looks like it has been transplanted from an English country village. It was indeed constructed here amid the green lawns of Churchill Park in 1887 by an English architect. On a small slope next to the church there is a sight that is guaranteed to hold your attention. Copenhagen has numerous fountains but this, the **Gefion Fountain**, is the city's most spectacular. It was commissioned by the Carlsberg Foundation, and in 1908 sculptor Anders Bundgaard's depiction of the legend of the Nordic goddess Gefion – who turned her four sons into oxen and used them to plough the island of Zealand out of Sweden – was unveiled.

> The Danes love sarcasm, even with complete strangers, and they appreciate it when you are sarcastic in return.

Follow the right-hand path through delightful gardens past the fountain for about 800 yards to Langelinie, until you arrive at the most famous statue of all, **Den Lille Havfrue (the Little Mermaid**; *see page 79*). In Andersen's fairytale, this tragic sea-girl exchanged her voice for human legs in order to gain the love of an earthly prince, but mutely had to watch as he jilted her for a real princess. In desperation, she threw herself into the sea and turned into foam. To the dismay of both visitors and Danes, the mermaid has frequently been vandalised – she has on different occasions lost her head and an arm. Luckily, the workshop of sculptor Edvard Eriksen retains the original moulds from 1913, and new parts can be cast if necessary. Although famous, it must be said that the Little Mermaid is rather small and appears insignificant compared to the photographs that often depict it at the mouth of the harbour.

After viewing the Little Mermaid, take the road running away from the water, cross a bridge and descend the flight of steps on the left. This leads to a wooden bridge on the far side

The Gefion Fountain, depicting the Nordic goddess and her four 'sons'.

of which is the **Kastellet (Citadel)**, a star-shaped fortress with five bastions. It was begun by Frederick III in 1662. Building continued until 1725 and today the fortress is still in use by the army – the church, prison and main guardhouse having resisted the assaults of time. It is a delightfully peaceful enclave, with a charming windmill (1847) and some remains of the old ramparts well worth seeing. Leave by another wooden bridge into Churchillparken and turn right onto Esplanaden. Continue west into Gernersgade and you are in the heart of Nyboder (new dwellings) whose long rows of yellow houses were built between 1631 and 1641 by Christian IV for his sailors. Painted yellow, with steep gabled roofs and shuttered windows, they form a fashionable, well-preserved community of homes still inhabited by navy personnel. A small museum, **Nyboders Mindestuer** (St Pauls Gade 24; open Wed 11am–2pm, Sun 11am–4pm; admission fee) contains the cramped 19th-century rooms of a typical family and a small naval exhibition.

Backtrack to Bredgade and turn right. The area from here to Kongens Nytorv is a residential quarter of substantial granite houses and quadrangles. Once very fashionable, the area was planned by architect Nicolai Eigtved at about the same time as Amalienborg. At number 70 there is a plaque commemorating the death of the philosopher Søren Kierkegaard in 1855. At number 68 you'll find the **Kunstindustrimuseet** (Museum of Decorative Art), a fine Rococo building and former 18th-century hospital *(see page 60)*.

Almost next door, at number 64, is Skt Ansgar Kirke, centre of the modest Roman Catholic community since 1842. A museum documents the history of Catholicism in the city since its virtual extinction in the Reformation of 1536. Immediately after the church stands the fascinating **Medicinsk-Historisk Museum** (Medical Museum; guided tours only, in English Jul–Aug Wed–Fri and Sun 1pm; admission fee). Then it comes as a surprise to see, across the road, the golden

One of Copenhagen's most recognisable icons: the Little Mermaid, caught between water and land at Langelinie.

onion-shaped domes of Alexander Nevsky Kirke, built for the Russian Orthodox community between 1881 and 1883.

A few steps further and the great dome of Frederikskirken, better known as **Marmorkirken** (Marble Church; open Mon–Fri 10am–5pm, Wed till 6pm, Sat–Sun noon–5pm; visits to the dome daily 1pm and 3pm precisely), rises high to your right. Measuring 31m (100ft) in diameter, this is one of the largest church domes in Europe. The cornerstone was laid by King Frederik V in 1749, however by 1770 the Norwegian marble required for the building had become so expensive that the project was halted, and it remained standing for a century as a picturesque ruin. It was eventually consecrated in 1894, the Norwegian marble having been complemented by Danish marble from Faxe.

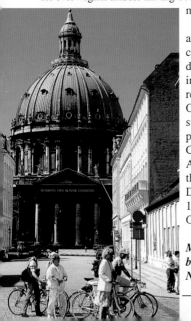

Inside, it's both impressive and beautiful. The dome, carried on 12 stout pillars, is decorated with rich frescoes in blue, gold and green – representing the Apostles. Outside, the church is surrounded by statues of personalities of the Danish Church, ranging from St Ansgar (who helped to bring the Christian religion to Denmark) to Grundtvig, the 19th-century educationalist. On the roof are 16 figures

Mighty Marmorkirken, built with Danish and Norwegian marble.

from religious history, from Moses to Luther. Proceed to Kongens Nytorv along Bredgade: the ever-changing array of boutiques, antiques shops and galleries will all compete for your attention.

UNIVERSITY QUARTER AND PARKS

From Rådhuspladsen, go west for a short way along Vester Voldgade and then turn right into narrow Studiestræde, the home to a melange of antiques shops, bookstalls and boutiques gathered in an 18th-century setting.

At Studiestræde 6 a plaque records that H.C. Ørsted, who discovered electro-magnetism in 1820, lived here. A few metres further on, at the corner of Nørregade, you will see one of Copenhagen's oldest preserved buildings, the former Bispegården (Bishop's Residence), built in 1500 and now part of the university. Nearby on Bispetorvet stands a monument erected in 1943 commemorating the 400th anniversary of the introduction of the Reformation to Denmark.

At the end of Studiestræde stands the **Domkirken** (Cathedral) of Copenhagen, known as **Vor Frue Kirke** (Church of Our Lady). Bishop Absalon's successor, Sunesen, is said to have laid its foundations in the 12th-century, but by 1316 it had already burned down four times. Later, two further constructions were destroyed – by the great 1728 fire and by British bombardment in 1807. The present church was reconstructed by V.F.K. and C.F. Hansen in 1811–29. Its large austere interior is relieved by a collection of heroic statues by Bertel Thorvaldsens: 12 massive marble Apostles line the aisle, while an orange-lit altar is surrounded by bronze candelabra and dominated by his figure of Christ.

Proceed along the left (north) side of the cathedral. On the left is the main Copenhagen University block, which dates back in its present form only as far as the 1830s. The university was founded in 1479. This is a typical student area with a number of interesting bookshops.

Turn right into Fiolstræde, a lively spot for alfresco dining and left into Skindergade which leads into **Gråbørdretorv** (Greyfriar's Square), a large, picturesque traffic-free square surrounded by brightly painted 18th-century houses. This was the site of a Franciscan monastery until the Reformation. Cafés and restaurants have proliferated here in recent years and of the latter one of the best is named after the square. This is also a pleasant place to sit and rest.

Exit at the far side of the square by Løvestræde, which almost immediately leads into Købmagergade. At the corner stands the **Post og Tele Museum** (Post and Tele-communications Museum; open Tues, Thurs–Sat 10am–5pm, Wed 10am–8pm, Sun noon–4pm; admission fee). The museum has an excellent roof-top café which offers great views of the city.

Turn left onto pleasant Købmagergade, which is one of Copenhagen's oldest commercial thoroughfares. Here Christian IV laid the cornerstone of **Trinitatis Kirke** (Trinity Church) in 1637 and built the **Rundetaarn** (Round Tower; *for opening times, see page 79*) in 1642 as an astronomical observatory. The Round Tower has been one of the city's most beloved landmarks for more than 350 years, even if it only reaches the modest height of 36m (118ft). It is more interesting to visit than the rather conventional church. You can walk to the top, but not by any ordinary means – steps would have been impractical for raising the heavy equipment needed here. Instead, a wide spiral ramp winds around for 210m (690ft) inside the tower. Not only did Tsar Peter the Great ride up to the top on horseback in 1716, but his empress followed him in a horse-drawn coach. The

Round and round you go – to reach the top of the Rundetaarn you must wind your way up a spiral ramp.

building across Købmagergade from the Round Tower, at the corner with Krystalgade, is the Regensen university hostel. Although students have lived here since 1623 most of the present structure dates from the 18th century. The notable addition is an arcade built in 1909. A couple of hundred metres along Krystalgade stands the synagogue of Copenhagen. It was inaugurated in 1833.

Backtrack on Krystalgade and continue past Trinity Church on Landemærket for two blocks. On the left, on Åbernå, music lovers will find an attraction certainly worth a visit: the **Musikhistorisk Museum** (Musical History Museum, Åbenrå 30; open May–Sept Fri–Wed 1pm–3.50pm, Oct–Apr Wed, Sat–Mon 1pm–3.50pm; admission fee) focuses on the history of musical instruments in Europe from 1000 to 1900. Landemærket soon terminates at busy Gothersgade. Turn right and then left onto Kronprinsessegade,

In the sunny summer months, Copenhagen's parks are awash with colour.

all the time skirting Kongens Have. On the right at No. 30 Kronprinsessegade is **Davids Samling** (David's Art Collection, *see page 69*).

Time to investigate the park, **Kongens Have**, that was laid out in 1606–34 when Christian IV announced that the Christiansborg Palace was becoming too official and oppressive. At that time he began to build a small country mansion for himself in a corner of the site, which was then situated beyond the town walls. This he eventually expanded into the most charming three-storey Dutch Renaissance-style **Rosenborg Slot** (Castle; *see page 79*)), which became home for the next three generations of kings until Frederik IV erected Frederiksberg Castle in 1710. After that date Rosenborg was only used occasionally and since 1838 it has been a royal museum of considerable grace and character and home of the crown jewels. Christian helped to plan the building, and it has all the frills and furbelows, turrets and towers, moats and battlemented gateways characteristic of a 'proper' castle, yet it retains the ambience of a weekend retreat.

The castle's 24 rooms are arranged chronologically, beginning with his tower room study – still furnished in its original style. The Long Hall, with tapestries of the Swedish Wars, ornate ceiling and three almost life-size silver lions, is not to be rushed through. In the hall is one of the world's largest collections of silver furniture, most of it from the 18th century.

The treasury, which is in the cellar, is home to the crown jewels. In addition to the oldest existing specimen of the Order of the Elephant *(see page 56)*, there are 18 cases full of crowns, gilded swords, precious stones and coronation cups – even royal inkwells and tea-sets in pure gold. The centrepiece of this regal room is the 17th-century crown of the absolute monarchy – made out of gold, with diamonds, two sapphires and ruby spinels. The park itself shouldn't be ignored either, on fine days it is always full of people enjoying themselves with typical Danish exuberance.

Gardeners will be particularly interested in the **Botanisk Have** (Botanical Gardens; open daily May–Sept 8.30am–6pm, Oct–Apr Tues–Sun 8.30am–4pm; admission free), located behind Rosenborg, across Øster Voldgade.

Art lovers should allow themselves time to explore the **Statens Museum for Kunst** (National Gallery), further north on Øster Voldgade *(see page 621)*. The gallery is particularly strong on 19th-century Danish landscapes, representative Dutch and Flemish works of art from Rembrandt to Paulus Potter, an Italian collection including Titian and Tintoretto, and perhaps the world's finest collection of Dürer prints. The stunning new wing, home to modern works and 25 Matisse canvasses, has aroused much controversy for its architecture.

Now, it's certainly possible to return to Rådhuspladsen by bus or, if you prefer, by train from Nørreport Station to Central Station. However, it isn't that far to walk and for those so willing there is another surprise on the way.

Tivoli

The concept of Tivoli derives from the 18th-century pleasure gardens that became popular in European cities. Their aim was to combine gardens, pavilions, music, entertainment, restaurants and other forms of amusements together in a tasteful and pleasing setting.

In 1843 the widely travelled, enterprising Georg Carstensen obtained a royal assent to establish such a pleasure garden, the Carstensen's Tivoli and Vauxhall Gardens. It was to be based upon one he had seen in Paris, and located just outside the city boundaries. Over the years Copenhagen has expanded greatly, and Tivoli – covering almost 83,000 sq m (nearly 21 acres) – has become an oasis of fun and pleasure in a busy 21st-century city. The gardens have been modernised, amusements have been updated, and many restaurants added, but these additions have always been made in such a way so as to retain the tradition and style. The original concept remains, and many of the favourites such as fireworks, performing artists, pantomimes and the internationally famous Tivoli Boys Guard date back to Tivoli's early years.

Tivoli is magical, its ambience created by both chance and inspiration. It's a reflection of the Danes' desire to enjoy themselves in pleasurable surroundings, a place for all the family and all generations to be together and have fun. As such, it is Denmark's most visited attraction, hosting nearly 4 million visitors a year, one-third of whom are not Danish. This makes it the third most visited amusement park in Europe. There is no single theme to Tivoli – it is multi-faceted – but the style is very much exotic and romantic and meant to inspire an atmosphere quite different from day-to-day life.

Expect to find the unexpected: Chinese-style pavilions, a variety of theatres which provide a stage for all events from international stars to pantomime, concert hall and everything in between. Amusements range from 25 large rides to the long-time favourite 'try-your-strength' machine (more than half of the rides are geared towards children). You will certainly never suffer from a lack of food or drink. There are nearly 40 different restaurants, some of which are of gourmet standard, and any number of snack bars, cafés and beer houses (more than 1,600,000 bottles of beer are consumed each year). You can even bring *smørrebrød* from the Vesterbrogade shops to a restaurant by the lake, buy some coffee, and freely use the plates, utensils and napkins.

There are 400,000 flowers blooming at any one time. After dark, trees and pathways are lit by more than 110,000 incandescent lamps that produce a soft warm glow. Free fireworks shows are an institution at Tivoli and the fireworks are produced and manufactured by Tivoli's own pyrotechnist.

In reality, it is impossible to clearly describe Tivoli in words as the intent of the park is to create a feeling; and it most certainly does. The feeling reflects wonderfully Danish characteristics – to peacefully eat, drink and be happy. In many other countries, so much free-flowing alcohol would be sure to cause problems, but they are infrequent here; when someone does get too rambunctious the inspectors take care of the matter swiftly and quietly.

Tivoli Gardens, Vesterbrogade 3; open daily mid-Apr–mid-Jun and late-Aug–late-Sept Sun–Wed 11am–11pm, Thurs and Sat till midnight, Fri till 1am; mid-Jun–late-Aug Sun–Thurs 11am–midnight, Fri and Sat 11am–1am; tel: 33 15 10 01; <www.tivoli.dk>; admission fee. The daily programme is listed on posters throughout the park. Look out for the famous Tivoli Christmas market from late-November until Christmas.

Past Nørreport Station, and on the right hand side of NørreVoldgade, there is the **Ørsteds Parken**. Although not often frequented by visitors its charms, including a large lake, are certainly not overlooked by the locals.

CHRISTIANSHAVN

Though there's so much to see within a small radius of Rådhuspladsen and Kongens Nytorv, it's worth spending a few hours just over the harbour channel, crossing the Knippelsbro bridge into **Christianshavn**. The name, which means Christian's Harbour, is derived from Christian IV, and the area looks like a slice of Amsterdam, reflecting the king's predilection for Dutch architecture.

Having crossed the Knippel Bridge you are on Torvegade. Turn right at the intersection with Strandgade and stroll to the somber **Christians Kirke**. Built in 1755 by Nicolai Eigtved, it possesses an unexpected interior layout with arched galleries reminiscent of an old-time music hall. Now backtrack and after crossing Torvegade continue on Strandgade until reaching the **Danish Centre for Architecture** (open daily 10am–5pm; tel: 32 57 19 30; <www.kulturnet.dk>), which is located in a former warehouse at Gammel Dok. The area has numerous 17th- and 18th-century houses with cobbled courtyards flanked by small living annexes. N.F.S. Grundtvig *(see page 19)* spent some years at number 4B. Living at number 6 in the early 18th century was Admiral Peter Wessel Tordenskjold – a Dano-Norwegian hero who won battles at sea but whose exuberant lifestyle ashore lost him many good neighbours. It's said that every time he called *skål* during his frequent banquets, a salute would be fired from two cannons at the main doorway, with many a sleepless night had by all until his death in a duel in 1720. A few hundred metres to the southeast beckons the distinctive twisted spire of the **Vor Frelsers Kirke** (Church of Our Saviour; open daily except during services, Apr–Aug 11am–4.30pm, Sep–Mar 11am–3.30pm; admission free; tower open Apr–Oct, admission fee). To reach the church, simply wander along the banks of the canals. The scenery is reminiscent of Nyhavn; this time, though, you will see Dutch-style warehouses, narrow houses and small bars all topped by hoists, and numerous multi-coloured boats.

Construction of this brick and sandstone church began in 1682, under the direction of Lambert van Haven, and it was consecrated in April 1696. Its most dominant exterior feature, an external spiralling staircase that twists around the tower four times, was designed by Lauridz de Thurah and was dedicated in August 1752. He is said to have been influenced at the time by the Sant'Ivo alla Sapienza church in Rome. A total of 400 steps, 150 on the outside, lead from the entrance of the church to the gilt globe and Christ figure on top of the spire, but you are only allowed the rare experience of this outdoor climb between April and October, and only in good weather. From ground level to the top of the flag it is a distance of 90m (295ft), making it almost three times as high as the Round Tower.

The inside of the church is of interest not simply because of the choir screen that is guarded by six wooden angels, nor because of the ornate white marble font supported by four cherubs – not even because of the altar dating from 1732, replete with allegorical statues and Dresden-like figures playing in the clouds – but because of the monumental organ, built in 1700 and several times remodelled, on the last occasion in 1965. Beautifully ornamented, the whole construction is supported by two large stucco elephants. Elephants are popular in Copenhagen; in fact, in 1693

The spire of Von Frelsers Kirke is mounted via spiralling exterior stairs.

Christian V made the Order of the Elephant Denmark's most prestigious order. The central vault of the church is decorated with a monogram of Christian V, the royal coat-of-arms and a chain of the Order of the Elephant.

Outside Our Saviour's turn left onto Prinsessegade and follow it along to a somewhat more esoteric experience. It is one that may not be to everyone's taste and its long dreary brick wall gives little clue as to what lies behind. This was formerly the site of the Bådsmandsstræde Barracks until, in 1971, a group of local people broke through and so began the **Christiania** free town. Altogether more than 1,000 people live and work in this rather rundown but none the less colourful environment, and although they don't pay rent they do pay for water and electricity. They provide for themselves with an eclectic collection of small restaurants, co-operative markets and art stalls. Being an 'alternative' society, soft drugs are the basis of the local economy. Although this curious area is safe enough during the day, most visitors will want to use caution after dark. Those wishing to know more about Christiania can join a guided walk, departing at 3pm on Saturday and Sunday from inside the entrances to Christiania (tel: 32 57 96 70; charge).

OUTLYING SIGHTS

A number 350S bus from Rådhuspladsen will take you first to the Amagermuseet and then on to the charming small community of Dragør. As many of the shops in the latter are open on Sunday in the summer months – they are mostly closed in Copenhagen – this is a good day to take the trip.

First, in an old farmhouse on the village street in Magleby you'll find the

> Elephants are popular in Denmark, ranging from the country's oldest honour, the 'Order of the Elephant', to the label of a popular beer.

Amagermuseet (Amager Museum; open May–Sept Tues–Sun noon–4pm, Oct–Apr Wed and Sun noon–4pm; admission fee). The kitchen and bedrooms are furnished in the old style with items donated by villagers from the surrounding area. The collection began in 1901 and the museum explains the reasons for the Dutch atmosphere that prevails over this area.

The Dutch connection started during the reign of Christian II (1513–23), when he invited a colony of Netherlands farmers to come and improve soil cultivation in the area, and to provide the royal table with 'as many roots and onions as are needed'. He gave the Dutch special privileges to live in Store Magleby, which for centuries was referred to as Hollænderbyen (Dutchmen's Town). They had their own judicial system and church (with services in Dutch or Low German only), and developed a bizarre local costume – derived from Dutch, Danish, and French styles – a large collection of which is on display at the museum.

Take the 350S bus again for the 2-km (1-mile) trip to the water's edge at **Dragør**, where the harbour is packed with small boats and the 18th-century village remains remarkably preserved. A maze of cobbled streets and alleyways leads off from the only traffic road. A walk among the charming half-timbered, thatched or tile-roofed cottages with their postage-stamp gardens provides a vivid impression of what life was like in those times.

Beside the harbour, a 1682 fisherman's cottage, the oldest house in the town, has been imaginatively converted into the **Dragør Museum** (open May–Sept Tues–Sun noon–4pm; admission fee) devoted to local seafaring history. From here, you can catch the bus back to Rådhuspladsen.

Rådhuspladsen now provides the starting point for a trip to **Grundtvig's Kirke** (Gruntvig's Memorial Church; open-late-Mar–late-Oct Mon–Sat 9am–4.45pm, Sun noon–4pm, late-Oct–late-Mar Mon–Sat 9am–4pm, Sun noon–1pm; admission free) in northwest Copenhagen. Here, a 25-minute journey from the centre on bus number 10, a total of six million bricks have been laid as a monument honouring the man who was once called Denmark's greatest son.

Founder of the Danish residential high schools, Nikolai Frederik Severin Grundtvig (1783–1872) was a renowned educationalist, austere parson and prolific hymn-writer. Grundtvigs Kirke, built in his memory, is also a monument to early 20th-century Danish architecture. The church's design by Peder Jensen-Klint is

Even the weeds around the water pump have charm in Dragør.

extraordinarily simple but effective. A few chosen masons, some of them employed from start to finish, carried out the project between 1921 and 1940. Everything is in pale-yellow brick: the 50-m (160-ft) tall tower and the vaults of the 22-m (72-ft) nave, all the stairs and pillars, the balustrades, altar and the pulpit. Stainless-steel organ pipes (4,800 of them) look down on a vast, uncluttered nave. It's a fitting tribute to a man who composed 1,400 hymns, and a national monument that is worth a visit.

MUSEUMS

Copenhagen has many museums, with more still in the planning stages. As hours may be subject to change and there's little consistency in admission charges, it is advisable to check the museum listing in the free *Copenhagen This Week* guide. It is also worth purchasing a **Copenhagen Card** *(see page 124)*, which offers free entry or substantial discounts for a large number of museums.

Amalienborg Palace Museum, Christian VIII's Palace

Amalienborg Plads (open Nov–Apr Tues–Sun 11am–4pm, May–Oct daily 10am–4pm; admission fee). Step into the private chambers of the Danish kings from Christian IX to the late Frederik IX and discover how the royal family lived between 1863 and 1972 *(see page 42)*.

Davids Samling (David's Art Collection)

Kronprinsessegade 30 (open Tues, Thurs–Sun 1pm–4pm, Wednesday 10am–4pm, closed 5 Jun; tel: 33 13 55 64; <www.davidmus.dk>; admission free). A major collection of Islamic art, in addition to art and crafts from European countries *(see page 50)*.

Den Hirschsprungske Samling
(Hirschsprung Collection)

Stockholmsgade 20 (open Wed–Mon 11am–4pm; tel: 35 42 03 36; <www.hirsch sprung.dk>; admission fee, Wed free). A delightful little museum devoted to 19th-century Danish painting, sculpture and decorative art. Heinrich Hirschsprung, a rich tobacco merchant, donated the works to the Danish state in 1902. Look out for the portraits and pristine landscapes of C.W. Eckersberg (1783–1853), a teacher at Copenhagen's Royal Academy whose meticulous style had a far-reaching influence. The romantic landscapes by Johan Lundbye date from the middle of the 19th century. A generation later, Peter Severin Krøyer worked to popularise social-realist themes, while a unique Impressionist style was being developed by Laurits Tuxen as a student in Paris.

Frihedsmuseet
(Museum of the Danish Resistance)

Churchillparken (open May–mid-Sept Tues–Sat 10am–4pm, Sun 10am–5pm, mid-Sept–Apr Tues–Sat 11am–3pm, Sun 11am–4pm; tel: 33 13 77 14; <www.nat mus.dk>; admission fee, Wed free). A graphic record of wartime tragedy and the eventual victory over the Germans *(see page XX)*.

Kunstindustrimuseet
(Museum of Decorative Art)

Bredgade 68 (open Tues–Fri 10am–5pm, Sat–Sun noon–4pm; tel: 33 18 56 56; <www.kunstindustrimuseet. dk>; admission fee). A large display of Danish and European decorative art, along with Oriental handicrafts dating from the Middle Ages to the present. Housed in an attractive Rococo building (a former hospital) dating from 1757.

Summer performances of Shakespeare (in Danish) are held in the splendid garden *(see page 45).*

Københavns Bymuseum (Copenhagen Museum)

Vesterbrogade 59 (open May–Sept Wed–Mon 10am–4pm, Oct–Apr 1–4pm; tel: 33 21 07 72 <www.kbhbymuseum. dk>; admission fee). Founded in 1901, the museum illustrates the history of Copenhagen from the Middle Ages to the present time in innovative displays. Also on show is the Søren Kierkegaard Samling, a collection of artefacts relating to the Danish philosopher.

Louis Tussauds Voksmuseum (Wax Museum)

Hans Christian Andersens Boulevard 22 (open daily mid-Apr to mid-Sept 10am–10pm; mid-Sept–mid-Apr 10am–6pm; tel: 33 11 89 00, <www.tussaud. dk>; admission fee). Wax models of famous Danish and foreign personalities.

Statens Museum for Kunst (The National Gallery)

Sølvgade 48-50 (open all year Tues, Thurs–Sun 10am–5pm, Wed 10am–8pm; tel: 33 74 84 94; <www.smk.dk>; admission fee, Wed free). Fine paintings from early Dutch to modern Danish, including a large Matisse collection, are housed in a light and airy building *(see page 51).*

Teatermuseet (Theatre Museum)

Christiansborg Ridebane 18 (open Tues–Thurs 11am–3pm, Sat–Sun 1–4pm; tel: 33 11 51 76; <www.teatermuseet.dk>; admisson fee). In an elegant terrace above the stables is an extraordinary theatre museum. The delightful little auditorium and galleries are packed with Danish and international theatrical relics – memorabilia of Ibsen, Anna Pavlova and Hans Christian Andersen, as well as playbills, costumes and photographs of the country's theatre history *(see page 35)*.

Tøjhusmuseet (Royal Arsenal Museum)

Tøjhusgade 3 (open Tues–Sun noon–4pm; tel: 33 11 60 37; <www.thm.dk>; admission fee). Attendants wearing three-cornered hats and knee-length red jackets greet you as you enter this vast building, constructed in 1598–1604 on the southeast side of Christiansborg. It is an appropriate setting for a museum housing one of Europe's most important

collections of military uniforms and historic equipment. Cannonballs are piled high like potatoes. Guns on display range from a 15th-century cannon of the time of Queen Margrete I to sophisticated new weapons. Old military planes are suspended from the roof, and upstairs there is a glittering display of uniforms and small arms *(see page 35)*.

EXCURSIONS

In a country of 44,030 sq km (16,630 sq miles), nature has ingeniously divided Denmark into a land of more than 450 islands so that you are never more than 50km (30 miles)

A day in the lush countryside surrounding Copenhagen provides a pleasant respite from the attractions of the city.

Gentle breezes waft in the summer air across the rolling green Danish countryside.

from the sea. Copenhageners have their own beach, woodlands and a wide lake area, and within the city boundary it is easy to organise an excursion. Options include boat trips, windmill and water-mill sightings, a visit to a royal country castle, and exploring traditional villages.

Open-Air Folk Museum and Lyngby Lake

At Sorgenfri, 16km (10 miles) north of the city, lies **Frilandsmuseet**, the intriguing Open-Air Folk Museum (open

Apr–Sept Tues–Sun 10am–5pm, Oct Tues–Sun 10am–4pm; admission fee, Wed free; tel: 33 13 44 11; <www.natmus.dk>; times may vary, so before setting out check opening hours and times of guided tours in English with the Copenhagen tourist information office, *see page 123*). The museum is accessible by car along the A3 and A5 main roads; by direct bus 184 from Nørreport terminus in town; or by S-train to Sorgenfri station. Another more interesting route is on the same train, but with a change at Jægersborg station to the little red one-coach train known as *Grisen* ('The Pig'). This will drop you at Fuglevad Station near the museum's back entrance.

Forty farmhouses, cottages, workshops and a Dutch-type windmill are scattered about the 35-hectare (90-acre) site of Frilandsmuseet – all furnished in the original style, even down to combs and portraits.

Broadly, the buildings are split into geographical groups laid out along country lanes, together with bridges and village pumps, and all are authentically landscaped. Each building has been transplanted, tile by tile, timber by timber, from its original location. You'll find a Zealand group, a Jutland and a Faroes group, etc. Homes of all classes are represented, from peasant to landowner, as well as artisan and farmer.

The smell of old timber and tar pervades the rooms. Geese and sheep are driven along the lanes. Displays of folk dancing, sheep shearing, threshing and weaving are given during the summer. There are horse-and-carriage rides and picnic spots in tree-lined meadows.

Allow yourself time during good weather to stroll a kilometre or so down the main road towards Lyngby, where you can take a rural boat ride scarcely equalled in any capital city. On your left is the white-walled baroque castle,

Sorgenfri Slot (closed to the public), built in the 18th-century by Lauridz de Thurah who also designed the spire of Vor Frelsers Kirke *(see page 55)*.

Proceed over Mølleåaen (the Mill Stream). Follow the signs to the right for Lyngby Sø-Bådfarten ('Lyngby Lake-Boat Trip') to find two venerable canopied boats at the quayside. These have plied the four lakes since the 1890s and offer visitors a most charming form of transport. A 45-minute cruise, either Lyngby–Frederiksdal or Lyngby–Sophienholm, gives you the chance to savour these delightful tree-covered backwaters and broad, reedy lakes. The boats operate from May until September or October, depending on the weather.

> *Hygge* – a peculiar and untranslatable Danish word represents the things Danes love most: family, friends, food, drink and happiness.

As you float by, you'll pass the 1803 mansion of Marien-borg amid the trees, the official summer residence of Danish prime ministers. Further on is Frederiksdal, with its castle on a hill above. This former royal house has been lived in by the same family since 1740.

An alternative trip will take you to Sophienholm Mansion (1805), now a community cultural arts centre. Outdoor café tables give an idyllic view over the waters of Bagsværd Sø.

Back on Lyngby quay, the 184 bus can take you directly back into town, or it's a short walk to Lyngby S-train station.

North Zealand and its Castles

Some 130km (around 80 miles) of sea views and castle turrets, beaches and rolling farmland is what you can expect if you set about touring northern Zealand.

The closest of these attractions to Copenhagen, just to the south of Humlebæk and easily accessible by train, is the **Louisiana Museum for Moderne Kunst** (Louisiana Modern Art Museum; open daily 10am–5pm, Wed until 10pm; admission fee; tel: 49 19 07 91; <www.louisiana.dk>). The museum is housed in the mid-19th-century mansion of a thrice-married cheese merchant whose wives were all named Louise. Airy white-washed galleries built into the hillside form the backdrop to an extensive collection, including works by Picasso, Warhol and Rauschenberg, the COBRA artists such as Asger Jorn, and more recently, Georg Baselitz and Per Kirkeby. A glazed

Outside the Louisiana Museum you can admire the sculptures and enjoy the view.

corridor leads past a group of Giacometti figures to the excellent Museum Café and a terrace featuring metal mobiles by Alexander Calder. In the gardens, you can sit on the lawns dotted with sculptures and marvel at Henry Moore's colossal bronze women silhouetted against the waters of the Øresund. There is a range of children's activities to grab the attention of young visitors to Louisiana, too.

Helsingør

Further north along the coast, and at the narrowest stretch of the Øresund, is Helsingør, also known as Elsinore. Again very easily reached by train from Central Station, here is an attraction that should not be missed. On leaving the station Helsingør's most famous landmark comes into view, the **Kronborg Slot** (Kronborg Castle; open May–Sept daily 10.30am–5pm, Apr and Oct Tues–Sun 11am–4pm, Nov–Mar Tues–Sun 11am–3pm; admission fee; tel: 49 21 30 78; <www.kronborgslot.dk>). To reach it on foot from the station takes about 20 minutes. Many people will be familiar with Kronborg as 'Hamlet's castle', made famous by the film version starring Laurence Olivier and Vivien Leigh.

The castle was built between 1574 and 1585 at the command of Frederik II for the purpose of extracting tolls from ships that were entering the narrow Sound, and thus the Baltic. Frederik had more than just a stronghold in mind. He built a castle that could be lived in, fortified with ramparts and bastions so that a number of large windows and decorated towers could be added with impunity. He sent for the Flemish architect Antonius van Opbergen to design the four-wing structure, then engaged various Danish and Dutch artists to paint, weave and indulge in decorative sculpture on a scale never before seen in Scandinavia.

The moated brick castle today stands as Frederik's proudest memorial, now sparsely furnished but immensely impressive. It has a feeling of solid strength and royal presence throughout, permeating the elaborate little chapel, the long galleries and stone stairways, and most of all the huge oak-beamed Banqueting Hall. At 64 x 11m (210 x 36ft), it is the largest hall of its kind in northern Europe and one of the noblest rooms of the Danish Renaissance. Decked out now with 12 paintings of the Øresund by Isaac Isaacsz, its

Kronborg Castle may be better known to Shakespeareans as Elsinore, though Hamlet himself never slept here.

walls were once hung with 42 tapestries by the Dutchman Hans Knieper, depicting the 111 Danish kings said to have reigned before Frederik II. Fourteen of the tapestries survive, of which seven are to be seen in a small room beneath the hall, and the remainder are in the National Museum in Copenhagen *(see page 36)*. Underneath the castle are

> **Danish bicycles come in every shape, size and form, including some with a big box on the front to carry children.**

extensive cellars and dungeons, but the most renowned exhibit at Kronborg, is the statue of Holger the Dane *(see page 13)*. In the castle's northern wing you'll discover the interesting **Handels-og Søfartsmuseet** (Trade and Maritime Museum; open May–Sept daily 10.30am–5pm, Oct and Apr Tues–Sun 11am–4pm; admission fee) with its display of navigation instruments, as well as relics from early Danish settlements in Greenland and elsewhere.

Helsingør has more to offer than the castle alone: there are medieval streets of colour-washed houses, the 15th-century Skt Mariæ Kirkes and a Carmelite Kloster (Convent) to see. A short ferry trip across the sound to Helsingborg, Sweden, is always of interest. If you visit Helsingør on Saturday, you will come face-to-face with a social phenomenon: Swedes by the thousands making the crossing to enjoy cut-price shopping in Denmark. High on their list is alcohol, their own laws being strict and the prices much steeper, and the shopkeepers of Helsingør are more than happy to oblige. As a consequence, stores selling spirits, wine and beer are prevalent, and it is a strange sight to see Swedes pushing around little two-wheeled trolleys with two cases of empty beer bottles. The number of cases is significant, as that is their duty-free limit, and the empty bottles will be replaced by full ones just before they embark for the sailing home.

The cottages at Helsingør are most humble in comparison to the elaborate Kronborg Castle nearby.

Visits to Helsingør and to the Louisiana Museum of Modern Art may be readily combined. On completing the Helsingør excursion, return to the railway station and board the train for Copenhagen. Alight at Humlebaek (the fourth stop); turn left on leaving the station and a 15-minute walk leads to the Louisiana museum.

Alternatively, at the bus terminal next to the railway station in Helsingør board a number 388 bus (there are two an hour) for the pleasant 20-minute journey along the coast before alighting at the museum entrance.

To return to Copenhagen from Louisiana turn left onto the main road and a 15-minute walk leads back to Humlebæk railway station, or you can catch a bus. Trains run regularly into the city centre.

Hillerød

Although Hillerød is just 9 km (5 miles) from Helsingør and it is possible to visit both places in the same day, it is not really recommended as time and train schedule constraints combine against such a trip. This means that, in reality, it will be necessary to reach the town by S-train from Copenhagen.

Worth a visit, Hillerød is the site of Denmark's architectural showpiece, Christian IV's grandest achievement, and one of the greatest Renaissance castles in northern Europe, **Frederiksborg Slot** (Frederiksborg Castle; National History Museum open daily Apr–Oct 10am–5pm, Nov–Mar 11am–3pm; tel: 48 26 04 39; <www.frederiksborgmuseet.dk>; admission fee; gardens open daily 10am, closing at different hours depending on the season).

Frederiksborg, an imposing Renaissance castle spanning three islands, is best reached by boat.

This picturesque brick and sandstone castle is dramatically situated across three islands on a lake, and the best way to reach it is by way of a small boat that departs from the city centre. Although the oldest parts of the castle date from around 1560 and were built by Frederik II, most of the castle dates from between 1600 and 1620, his son, Christian IV's, era. The style is Dutch Renaissance, and the result is spectacular. Danish monarchs resided here for about a century, and beginning in 1671 the absolute monarchs were crowned in the palace chapel.

In 1859 much of the interior was destroyed by fire, but between 1860 and 1884 it was rebuilt with financial support from first the brewer J.C. Jacobsen and later the Carlsberg Foundation. Since 1878 the castle has been the home of the Danmarks Nationalhistoriske Museum (National History Museum). This occupies more than 60 rooms and contains a complete record of the Danish monarchy, beginning with Christian I, who established the Oldenburg line (1448–1863), through all the monarchs of the following Glücksburg line, right down to the present queen, Margrethe II. Although the exhibits are of interest, the actual rooms of the castle are more so.

Riddersalen (the Knights' Hall) and the chapel are Frederiksborg's ultimate triumph. The 55-m (185-ft) Knights' Hall is awesome in its dimensions, with tapestried walls, marble floor and carved wooden ceiling, all reconstructed from old drawings after the 1859 fire.

Below the Knights' Hall, Slotskirken (the chapel) escaped the fire, leaving its stunning gilt pillars and high vaulted nave virtually untouched. Almost every inch here is richly carved and ornamented. The chapel has inset black marble panels with quotations from the scriptures, marquetry panels in ebony and rare woods, and both its altar and pulpit in ebony with biblical scenes in silver relief. The organ is one of Europe's most notable, an almost unchanged original from 1610 by the Flemish master Esaias Compenius.

Around the gallery of this chapel the window piers and recesses are hung with coats-of-arms belonging to knights of both the orders of the Elephant and the Grand Cross of Danneborg. Some modern recipients are also represented, such as Sir Winston Churchill and General Eisenhower.

Roskilde

With an 800-year-old cathedral housing the splendid tombs of 37 monarchs, with Viking ships salvaged from the fjord and now presented in a splendid maritime museum, **Roskilde** has plenty to offer those who undertake the short train journey from Copenhagen centre.

Upon arrival, head straight for the centre of this small, neat town and for the three green spires which dominate the flat landscape for miles about. This is **Domkirke** (the Cathedral; open Apr–Sept Mon–Sat 9am–4.45pm, Sun and holidays 12.30pm–4.45pm, Oct–Mar Tues–Sat 10am–3.45pm, Sun and holidays 12.30pm–3.45pm; admission fee).

One of the most remarkable buildings in Denmark, it began life as a wooden church built by King Harald Blacktooth around AD 1000, when he first converted to Christianity. In the 1170s, Bishop Absalon, founder of Copenhagen *(see page 12)*, built a brick-and-stone cathedral here for his new bishopric, and during the course of the next 300 years this grew into the Romanesque-Gothic amalgam of today.

Christian IV added the distinctive spires in 1635. He also erected his own burial chapel and a gilded royal pew in the north wall of the church, heavily latticed and shielded from public view so that (it is said) he could smoke his pipe in

The dominant spires of Roskilde Domkirken, home of an eclectic array of tombs of Danish kings.

peace during Sunday services. Nearly all the Danish kings and queens since Margrete (who died in 1412) are buried here in sarcophagi and chapels all different from one another in a jumbled symphony of style.

On the south side, the chapel of King Frederik V is a simple design in white paint and Norwegian marble, with 12 tombs grouped around it. In contrast, the Christian IV chapel on the north side is marked by elaborately wrought ironwork from 1618 and interior decoration mainly from the 19th century featuring frescoes, paintings depicting scenes from his reign, and bronze statues.

A light note is introduced by the clock high on the southwest wall of the nave: as each hour arrives, St George and his horse rear up, beneath them a dragon utters a shrill cry, a woman figure strikes her little bell four times with a hammer and a man rings his big bell once. The chapel on the outside of the cathedral beside the northwestern tower was inaugurated in 1985 and dedicated to the memory of Frederik IX, the king of Denmark from 1947–72, who is buried here.

To the front of the church is Stændertorvet, the traditional square of this old market town, lined with outdoor café tables in good weather, and fruit and vegetable stalls every Wednesday and Saturday morning. On Saturday there is also a popular flea market.

To the rear is some public parkland, where you can walk down to the fjord and **Vikingeskibshallen** (the Viking Ship Museum; open daily May–Sept 10am–5pm, Oct–Apr, 10am–4pm; admission fee). When 11th-century Danes wanted to block off the sea-route to Roskilde from the ravaging Norwegians, they sank five Viking ships across a narrow neck of the shallow fjord here. These ships, salvaged in 1962, now form the basis of the Viking Ship Museum and are superbly displayed. They include a warship of the type portrayed in the Bayeaux Tapestry and an awe-inspiring longship, the dreaded man o' war, immensely seaworthy and used for long-range raiding.

The museum building stands on the edge of the water with one side made completely of glass, bringing the fjord almost into its main room. The outline of each ship was first reconstructed in metal strips, then the thousands of pieces of wood were placed in position after treatment. The museum is lavishly illustrated with photographs and charts, and free film shows are put on for the public in the cinema cellar, recounting (in English) the full story of the salvage.

In recent years the Vikingeskibshallen has been developed into a fascinating complex in which you can see wooden

Vikingeskibshallen houses five 11th-century Viking ships, plus other exhibits illuminating this remarkable find.

boats being built by hand using the original skills, go out for a sail on one of these wooden vessels, and eat in the attractive restaurant.

Then, to end the day in a truly Viking flavour, you can sample a draught of the favourite brew of these hardy sailors, *mjød* (mead).

Roskilde is a charming town in its own right, and has a few other museums of peripheral interest. Although more than 1,000 years old, it is probably most known internationally for the **Roskilde Festival** <wwwroskilde-festival.dk>, a major, rock-and-roll summer musical festival held annually for more than 30 years. It features top international stars.

Copenhagen Highlights

Christiansborg Slotsplads (Christiansborg Palace): tel: 33 92 64 92; <www.slotte.dk>; this is the sixth castle to be constructed over Bishop Absalon's original 12th-century edifice, the ruins of which can be visited in the basement. The complex is home to the Danish Parliament *(Folketing)*, Danish Supreme Court, Royal Reception Chambers *(see page 34)* – the setting for a series of 11 tapestries, known as Les Gobelins – Royal Stables, Theatre Museum, Thorvaldsen Museum and the Arsenal Museum *(see page 35)*.

Nationalmuseet (National Museum): Ny Vestergade 10 (open Tues–Sun 10am–5pm; tel: 33 13 44 11; <www.natmus.dk>; admission fee, free Wed). The biggest museum in Scandinavia is a treasure trove of artefacts, from Stone Age rock carvings and Mongolian tents to Danish domestic interiors showing how people have lived since the 17th century *(see page 36)*.

Ny Carlsberg Glyptotek: Dantes Plads 7 (open Tues–Sun 10am–4pm; tel: 33 41 81 41; <www.glyptotek.dk>; admission fee, Wed and Sun free). The outstanding classical collection of Danish brewer Carl Jacobsen is brought together under one elaborate roof; exhibitions of Egyptian, Greek, Roman and Etruscan art are featured alongside later French paintings and sculpture, including 73 bronze statuettes by Degas *(see page 38)*.

Amalienborg Slotsplads (Amalienborg Palace): Four elegant Rococo palaces that have been home to the Danish Royal Family since the 1750s; the changing of the guard at noon is not to be missed. The palace is closed to the public, but a museum in Christian VIII's palace gives a glimpse of late-19th-century royal life *(see pages 41 and 59)*.

Den Lille Havfrue (The Little Mermaid): Langelinie. Edvard Eriksen's bronze sculpture of Andersen's Little Mermaid gazing wistfully out to sea is emblematic of Copenhagen, and is its most famous statue. Visitors will be surprised at how small this is, especially when compared with the cleverly angled photographs in all the guide books *(see page 43)*.

Rundetaarn (Round Tower): Købmagergade 52A (open Jun–Aug Mon–Sat 10am–8pm, Sun noon–8pm; Sept–May Mon–Sat 10am–5pm, Sun noon–5pm; tel:33 73 03 73; <www.rundetaarn.dk>; admission fee). The astronomical observatory built by Christian IV in 1642 is one of Copenhagen's distinctive landmarks; access to the top of the tower is by a unique 209 m (687 ft) spiral ramp *(see page 48)*.

Rosenborg Slot (Rosenborg Castle): Øster Voldgade 4A (open Jan–Apr Tues–Sun 11am–2pm, May and Sept daily 10am–4pm, Jun–Aug daily 10am–5pm, Oct 11am–3pm; tel: 33 15 32 86; <www.rosenborg-slot.dk>; admission fee). Christian IV's elegant Dutch Renaissance palace is a dazzling showcase for exhibits from 500 years of Danish royal history; highlights include the crown jewels and magnificent Long Hall *(see page 50)*.

Tivoli Gardens: Vesterbrogade 3 (open daily mid-Apr–mid-Jun and late-Aug–late-Sept Sun–Wed 11am–11pm, Thurs and Sat till midnight, Fri till 1am; mid-Jun–late-Aug Sun–Thurs 11am–midnight, Fri and Sat 11am–1am; tel: 33 15 10 01; <www.tivoli.dk>; admission fee). Opened in 1843, this old-time pleasure park remains a perennial favourite for Danes and tourists alike. It offers a truly Danish combination of fun in the form of amusements, theatrical performances, concerts, fun fair, fireworks displays and numerous eateries from hot dog stands to gourmet restaurants, all set in beautiful gardens in the centre of Copenhagen *(see page 52)*.

WHAT TO DO

SHOPPING

Shopping in Copenhagen is a quality experience, and the city's pedestrian precincts and attractive squares add to the pleasure of seeking out those special purchases. A host of interesting shops in the pleasant side streets and arcades around the Strøget area specialise in everything from antiques to avant-garde furniture, while established department stores such as Illum and Magasin du Nord offer the very best in Danish design.

Shopping Hours

Shops are generally open from 9am or 10am–5.30pm or 7pm, Monday–Friday, and from 9am–1pm or 2pm on Saturday. However, shopping hours have been legally extended permitting stores to open from 6am–8pm if they so choose. A small number of shops (often food shops) are closed on Monday or Tuesday.

Certain stores stay open longer. These include bakers, florists, *smørrebrød* shops and kiosks. In addition, late-night (until 10pm or midnight) and Sunday shopping is possible at Central Station, which is like a cheery village with a supermarket, banks open for foreign exchange, a post office, room-reservation service and snack bars.

Where to Shop

Undoubtedly the place to begin is Strøget, a charming pedestrian-only combination of four streets starting at Rådhuspladsen with Frederiksberggade, which leads into Nygade Vimmelskaftet, Amergertorv, Østergade, and ends in Kongens Nytorv square. Along Strøget, said to be the longest

Copenhagen's streets, friendly to both bicycles and pedestrians, help make shopping a very pleasant experience.

pedestrian-only street in the world, you will find everything you could possibly want, and much more. The finest ceramics, silver and crystal shops, superb home furnishings and interiors stores, the city's leading furriers, antiques shops, department stores, clothing shops and souvenir outlets exist harmoniously, side-by-side with a varied selection of restaurants and bars.

In the smaller streets branching off (and parallel to) Strøget are an eclectic array of workshops belonging to young potters and silversmiths, numerous antiques shops, and many boutiques. On the opposite side of Kongens Nytorv, and convenient for those visiting Amalienborg and the Marble Church, are Bredgade and Store Kongensgade, with their extensive collection of boutiques, galleries and more antiques shops.

Instruments in the making – the art of music begins with design and craft.

Look out for a copy of the booklet *Funshopping København*. It will point you in the right direction for nearly 300 shops, restaurants, bars and hotels that you might otherwise miss.

VAT, or sales tax (in Danish MOMS), is 25 percent on all products and services. Foreign visitors who make large purchases (minimum 300kr in any one store) in outlets that display 'Tax-Free Shopping' stickers will be given a form to reclaim the VAT when they leave the country. Ask for details in the shop, *see page 119*, or check out the website <www.globalrefund.com/denmark>.

Good Buys

Royal Copenhagen is the collective name for a group of upmarket shops located in attractive historic buildings in the heart of Strøget at numbers 4, 6, 8 and 10 Amagertorv. These are the department store Illums Bolighus for the ultimate in modern design, home furnishings and accessories, Georg Jensen Silver, Royal Copenhagen Crystal, Royal Copenhagen Antiques and Georg Jensen Museum and Royal Copenhagen Porcelain. The last of these, founded in 1775, is world-famous for its porcelain. The secret of its poetic effect is an underglaze technique that allows landscape pastels, and even accurate skin colours, to be reproduced. Blue motifs come out particularly well. All the pieces are hand-painted after a quick first firing, then fired again for glazing at 1,400°C (2,600°F). No two pieces are alike.

Also of interest is the one-hour guided tour of the Royal Copenhagen factory at Smallegade 47, Frederiksberg – just a short bus ride from the city centre – and the opportunity to purchase products from the factory shop.

Amber jewellery is offered everywhere, particularly in stores along Strøget. The local 'gem' (actually a fossil resin from the southern Baltic) may be cheaper here than at home but beware, the quality can vary tremendously. Visit the House of Amber at Ravhuset, Kongens Nytorv 2.

Antiques are in plentiful supply, especially the homespun rather than the fine-art variety. The most likely shops to try are in the Old Town area.

Aquavit *(akvavit)*, the local spirit, usually flavoured with caraway seed, is cheaper than imported spirits. You'll find the best prices at the airport duty-free store.

Cigars, pipes and tobacco can be found in abundance in W.Ø. Larsen's delightful and beautiful shop at Amagertorv 9. In business for 400 years, it is the largest pipe shop in Copenhagen, and also has a fine selection of Cuban and other cigars.

Crystal glassware and porcelain products are especially good buys to take home if you want top-quality design matched with excellent craftsmanship. There is still a thriving tradition of blown glass, and, at Peter Svarrer, Kronprinsessegade 34B, you can watch skilled craftsmen at work on their exquisite and colourful creations. Of the numerous shops offering fine porcelain and crystal Skandinavisk Glas, Ny Østergade 4 – just off Østergade near Kongens Nytorv, <www.skandinaviskglas.com> – not only has a wide range of Scandinavian brands, but also specialises in fine crystal and porcelain from major European factories.

Down comforters. Once used these comforters will not easily be forgotten. Ofelia, Amagertorv 3 (opposite the Royal Copenhagen complex on Strøget) has a wide range of comforters and duvets as well as other products – such as down slippers – which will keep your feet nice and warm throughout the winter months.

Household furnishings. Danish furniture ranks among the world's best. Here you'll see items credited to the designer rather than to the factory. Furniture is a national pride and most good pieces will have a black circular 'Danish Furniture-Makers' sticker attached. Lamps are also lovingly designed, as are household textiles and hand-woven rugs. The best stores for interior furnishings are: Illums Bolighus, Strøget, <www.royalshopping.com>, and Casa, Store Regnegade 2, <www.casagroup.com>.

Knitwear comes Nordic-style, often highly patterned, warm, and, in some cases, expensive. There are knitwear shops all over the city; some sell wool and patterns for those who are tempted to set about knitting their own garments, but the Sweater Market, Frederiksberggade 15, just a few minutes from Rådhuspladsen along Strøget, claims to be Europe's largest sweater store.

Stainless-steel household products. Danish and other Scandinavian knives and flatware are of the highest standard and Zwilling J. A. Henckels A/S, Vimmelskaftet 47, has by far the widest and most interesting array.

Stereo equipment. The very latest in stereo systems, CD players, radios, and TV sets can be found at the Bang & Olufsen Centre, Østergade 3–5, near Kongens Nytorv.

Silver is another Danish speciality, dominated by the name Georg Jensen. Silver in Denmark is quality-controlled and should always be hallmarked. The Jensen showrooms at Amagertorv 4 offer creations that range from key rings to highly precious jewellery.

Souvenirs are myriad. Little mermaid figures, Copenhagen dolls in frilly skirts and black lace caps, blue ceramic figurines and animals, and countless trolls and Vikings abound, as well as hand-painted spoons, racks, and pepper-mills. A particularly attractive Danish keepsake is an Amager shelf – a group of three or four small hand-painted shelves in a triangular frame that hangs on the wall. Beware, however, of cheap versions.

Street artists provide some local colour at Town Hall Square on Amager Island.

Toys are simple and attractive, especially those in solid wood. You'll also see hundreds of the Danish wooden soldiers in all sizes. Many new stores such as Krea (Vestergade 4–6) have opened up, which specialise in educational toys for children of all ages.

Clocks and watches, etc. Gullacksen Ure, Frederiksberggade 8 on Strøget, may not be the largest of such shops, but its owner is the third generation of an old watchmaker family. Besides a wide selection of Danish and international brand-name watches, clocks, barometers and hygrometers,, look for the museum pieces on the walls. Of particular interest are the stylish, and very practical, Jacob Jensen temperature stations.

ENTERTAINMENT

When in Copenhagen, relax as the Danes do. Rent a bike for a different view of life, walk in the beech woods and parks, have a night on the town at a concert or jazz club – or simply pause for a snack on one of the many public benches.

Botanical gardens. Avid gardeners could happily pass two or three days examining the 70 formal areas, the palm house and various other greenhouses on the 10-hectare (24-acre) Botanisk Have site opposite Rosenborg Castle, <www.botanic-garden.ku.dk>. It opens daily until sunset all year. Get there by bus 6A from Rådhuspladsen.

Café society. Another way of life altogether – relaxed and very welcoming. Sit as long as you like over a beer or coffee, gaze at the eccentric décor, and take time out to meet the Danes. There are several especially friendly bars in the area around the university.

Cycling. Some hotels lend bicycles to their guests at no charge. Otherwise they're easy to hire *(see page 105)*. You can use the extensive network of cycle paths *(cykelsti)* without any worry about cars, or indeed the weather – if it starts raining, country buses and trains will carry your bike and taxis have bicycle racks.

Nightlife

Music, opera, ballet. Scores of concerts are held throughout the year at the Royal Theatre, Tivoli, the Royal Conservatory of Music, Radio House, in churches and museums. The Royal Danish Ballet is internationally acclaimed, and rightly so – it is one of Europe's oldest with a repertory going back 200 years. Nowadays, the company experiments in modern dance as well, but its great tradition lies in Bournonville classics, such as La Sylphide and *The Dancing School*, which are worth a going to see. The company performs from September to June.

Jazz, folk, rock. Copenhagen is one of Europe's leading jazz centres. Various clubs offer jazz for all persuasions every night until 2am or later. Many foreign stars now live in Denmark and appear at the top clubs. At smaller bars the jazz is free. There are several venues for folk music in the town centre, near the university. Rock music events frequently appear in the regular Copenhagen listings. On summer Sundays free rock concerts are held in Fælled Park. An annual two-week Jazz Festival is held at the beginning of July.

Nightclubs. There is a plethora of bars (open late) that serve as nightclubs, with the emphasis firmly on entertainment.

Discos. The usual routine for entrance into a Copenhagen disco is to enroll as a member at the door. Almost every variety of dance hall, from simple discotheques to sophisticated hotel nightclubs, is on offer and all are welcoming to visitors.

Cinemas. Films are shown in their original language with Danish subtitles or, increasingly, in Danish.

At home. If you are fortunate enough to be invited to a Danish home, don't turn down the opportunity. The Danes love to entertain and set great store by creating a cosy yet chic atmosphere for their guests.

Copenhagen by night. Copenhagen is well known for its more risqué entertainment and red-light district. This is now located in the rather unobtrusive Istedgade/ Halmtorvet area to the west of the Central Station.

Casino. Casino Copenhagen, Radisson Hotel, 77 Amager Boulevard; tel: 33 96 59 96; <www.casinocopenhagen.dk>.

SPORTS

There are plenty of sporting activities to suit every taste within easy reach of the city. The top spectator sport is football, while popular participation sports include sailing and fishing. Ask the nearest Danish tourist office *(see page 123)* for an up-to-date list of what's available.

Fishing. Jutland is the Danish mecca for sea fishing, but you can still go for Øresund cod, mackerel, gar-pike, or flat-fish from Amager and the coast to the north of the city. No special permit is required for fishing in Denmark, either in its

Entertainment in Copenhagen ranges from the sublime beauty of the Royal Danish Ballet (left) to the hard-hitting exuberance of the Jazz Festival (above).

lakes or rivers – a real boost to anglers. You can rent licensed boats on Lyngby, Furesø and Bagsværd lakes on the north-west edge of Copenhagen.

Football. The Danish football team competes at the highest level, and the sport has an enthusiastic following. The main Copenhagen stadium is at Idrætsparken, and is often used for major international matches.

Horse racing. The race track *(Galopbane)* at Klampenborg is open mainly on Saturdays from mid-April–mid-December. To get there, take the S-train to Klampenborg, then bus 160.

Sailing. Join enthusiasts sailing on the Øresund and inland lakes. Yachts and cruisers are available for hire. Evidence of

Windsurfing and other watersports are popular in summer on the seas off Copenhagen.

navigational proficiency is required for sailing on the Øresund, where a close watch must be kept for the constant ferry traffic. Book in advance with help from your local Danish tourist office *(see page 123).*

Skating. Numerous stretches of water within the capital's boundaries freeze up in winter and outdoor rinks are set up in the city centre, such as at Kongens Nytorv. There are also indoor rinks *(skøjtehal)* at Copenhagen Forum and other suburban locations (open Oct–Apr)

Swimming. There is good sea bathing along the Zealand coast north and south of Copenhagen, but the sea is rarely warm. Nude bathing is mainly at Tisvildeleje, away from the north coast. There are about a dozen indoor swimming pools in Copenhagen, some with sauna/massage and gym facilities, and several outdoor pools which are open from mid-May until the end of August. So successful has the clean up of the Inner Harbour been that each bank is now home to an outdoor swimming pool. Havnefronten is on the south waterfront at Islands Brygge while Havneholmen is on the north waterfront near the Fisketorvet shopping complex (open Jun–Aug, 11am–5pm).

Watersports. Water-skiing is popular on the Furesø, and it is possible to windsurf in Vedbæk harbour; contact Vedbæk Surfer Club, tel: 215 66 01 18, or consult the tourist office for details.

CHILDREN'S COPENHAGEN

Amusement parks. Tivoli *(see page 52)* should certainly appeal to the entire family. Less well known than Tivoli – and generally considered to be a rather downmarket version – is Bakken (tel: 39 63 35 44, <www.bakken.dk>), which is very popular with Danes. Situated on the outskirts of Klampenborg, just a 12-minute train ride from the city centre, it has approximately 100 rides, 35 cafés and restaurants and the country's most famous revue show. Entry is free.

Museums and attractions. Ripley's Believe it or Not Museum (Rådhuspladsen 57, tel: 33 91 89 91, <www.ripleys.dk>) houses a collection of 'bizarre but true' exhibits. Louis Tussaud's Wax Museum (HC Andersens Boulevard 22, tel: 33 11 89 00, <www.tussaud.dk>) has 200 wax effigies of celebrities. The Tycho Brahe Planetarium (Gammel Kongeve, tel: 33 12 12 24, <www.tycho.dk>) has a space theatre and a star store. The Experimentarium Science Centre (Tuborg Havnevej 7, tel: 39 17 33 33, <www.experimentarium.dk>) is a place where children are positively encouraged to tinker around with exhibits. At Christiansborg children can visit the Royal Stables *(see page 35)* and see the coaches and the horses that pull them.

Several major museums have special sections for children. These include the National Museum *(see pages 36, 78)*, the National Gallery *(see pages 51, 61)* and the Louisana Museum *(see page 67)*. The Royal Danish Naval Museum (Orlogsmuseet; Overgaden Oven Vandet 58, tel: 32 54 63 63; <www.orlogmuseet.dk>) features a magnificent display of model ships, a children's playroom and a replica submarine into which kids can climb. The Viking Ship Museum at Roskilde *(see page 76)* has a children's section where two Viking ships may be boarded.

Copenhagen's Zoologisk Have (tel: 72 20 02 80, <www.zoo.dk>), established more than 120 years ago, is widely considered to be one of the best zoos in Europe. It houses more than 2,500 animals and has a splendid children's section, restaurant and cafeteria. It's a 10-minute ride from Rådhuspladsen by bus 6A. Approximately 10km (6 miles) from the city centre, at Charlottenlund, is Danmarks Akvarium (tel: 39 62 32 83; <www.danmarks-akvarium.dk>), one of the largest and most beautiful aquariums in Europe.

Swimming. Indoors, the Vandkulturhuset (Water Culture House) at the DGI sports centre (Tietgensgade 65, tel: 33 29 80 59, <www.dgi-bye.dk>) is a state-of the-art swimming complex with facilities for children of all ages. Outdoors, the newly opened two Inner Harbour swimming pools *(see page 91)* have children's pools. Adjacent to the pool at Islands Brygge is a skateboarding park.

Tours. Almost anything to do with water appeals to youngsters, and organised canal trips are a must *(see page 114)*. Also worth considering are boat cruises including a voyage aboard a Viking vessel that departs from Roskilde *(see page 77)* and cruises from Lyngby *(see page 65)*.

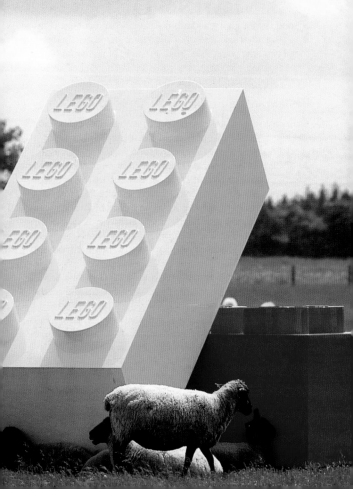

EATING OUT

Food is of a high standard in Denmark, and counts as little short of an obsession. Danes at home will happily spend two hours over their *frokost* (lunch) or up to four hours if entertaining special guests, while a *middag* (dinner) in celebratory mood can last from 6pm to very, very late.

Restaurants and Bars

There are more than 2,000 assorted restaurants, cafés, bars and snack bars in Copenhagen. Restaurants often serve a special dish of the day *(dagens ret)* and what is known as the *dan-menu* – a two-course Danish lunch or dinner for a fixed price – in addition to *à la carte* items. Keep an eye open for a *daglig kort* (daily menu), which usually features less expensive dishes than those listed on the more formal menu *(spisekort)*. You'll also find little lunch-only, cosy cellar restaurants listed in *Copenhagen This Week (see page 118)*. These offer good value with an old-world charm, and are frequented by Danes themselves. Copenhagen has more than its fair share of fine restaurants, and in 2003 had no fewer than six that had been awarded one Michelin star and another that had received two.

For a drink (at practically any time of the day or night – opening hours are particularly liberal), drop into one of the numerous cafés, pubs or bars dotted throughout the city.

VAT and service charges are included in the bill. Danes are not tip-minded, although after a meal you may want to round up your bill.

Breakfast

Breakfast *(morgenmad)* in a Danish hotel is a far cry from the Spartan 'continental breakfast' of a roll and a cup of

*Soak up the beautiful weather at one of Copenhagen's
many delightful pavement cafés.*

coffee. Bread rolls, meat, cheese, jam, pastries and probably
eggs are all accompanied by milk and fruit juice followed by
tea or coffee.

Cold Dishes

Cold food is Denmark's truly outstanding culinary
speciality, which you can soon learn to enjoy. *Smørrebrød*
(open sandwiches) are thickly buttered slices of rye or white
bread covered with one of a wide array of delicacies on
display: liver pâté *(leverpostej)*, beef tartare *(bøf tatar)*, veal
(kalvekød), ham *(skinke)*, roast beef *(stege oksekød)*, salmon
(laks), smoked eel *(røget ål)*, shrimp *(reje)*, cod roe
(torskerogn), herring *(sild)*, a variety of salads *(salat)* or

cheese *(ost)*. This main layer is garnished with various accessories that have been carefully chosen to enhance both taste and appearance. Larger restaurants have scores of different *smørrebrød*. The usual procedure is to mark your orders on the menu itself, specifying which kind of bread you want *(knækbrød*: crispbread; *rugbrød*: rye; *franskbrød*: white; *pumpernikkel*: black).

Don't confuse your *smørrebrød* with the Swedish word *smörgåsbord*, which has gained international currency as a description of the Scandinavian cold buffet-style spread, better known in Denmark as *det store kolde bord* (the cold table). There can be a bewildering array of dishes. For a fixed price, you start at one end of the table, helping yourself to herring in various forms, seafood, salads and other delicacies, and go on to sample liver pâté, ham and other cuts of meat. Despite

its name, the cold table always includes a few hot items, such as meatballs, pork sausages, soup and fried potatoes. Several kinds of bread and salads are also provided. Danish *akvavit (see page 83)* and beer go especially well with *koldt bord*.

Fish and Shellfish

Fish (or small canapés) is the traditional first course of a full meal. It is also avail-

A good meal and a view of the city from the Radisson SAS Royal Hotel.

able as a main course, and a great variety of fish appear on the Danish menu. Herring is one of the firm favourites, and may be served pickled, marinated or fried, with a sherry, vinegar, curry or fennel dressing. Succulent red Greenland shrimps are also popular. Lobster is widely offered – though it is not cheap – as is crab, cod and halibut.

Plaice features frequently in the local cuisine and may be served boiled or fried with a garnish of shellfish or parsley. You'll see the little Øresund *rødspætte* (red-spot plaice) on every menu. In summer, a speciality is *danske rejer*, small pink shrimps from local waters that are served piled high on white bread.

One great Scandinavian delicacy is *gravad laks*, in which raw salmon is pressed with salt and a small amount of sugar, and then sprinkled generously with chopped dill. A creamy sauce of oil, mustard and sugar is traditionally served alongside as an accompaniment.

Meat and Poultry

Although Danish meat dishes most frequently make use of pork and veal, beef has made a major breakthrough, as Danish farmers now breed more cattle. The kinds of steak that you are most likely to be offered are *fransk bøf*, fillet steak served with herb butter and French fries, and *engelsk bøf*, fillet steak served with fried onions and potatoes.

The top restaurants cook in classic French/international style. In small establishments, some typical Danish hot dishes appear on the menu such as *mørbradbøf*, a delectable legacy of the pork-only days – small cuts of tenderloin, lean, very tasty and served as a main course with boiled potatoes, onions and gravy.

More ordinary fare – but delicious nevertheless – are Danish meatballs *(frikadeller)*, a finely minced mixture of pork and veal, often served with potato salad and red cabbage. *Biksemad* is also cheap and tasty: a Danish hash of diced potatoes, meat and onions with a fried egg on top. A hearty Danish stew is *Hvids labskovs*, made from chunks of beef boiled with potatoes, peppercorns and bay leaves.

Chicken is most often served roasted with potatoes fried in butter and a cucumber salad *(agurkesalat)*. Roast duck comes with apple or prune stuffing and is usually accompanied by caramelised potatoes and a generous array of vegetables.

Salads

The word for salad, *salat*, has two meanings. It can be the familiar side dish of fresh lettuce, tomato, sliced egg and plentiful red peppers; or, more often, it's one of several mayonnaise mixtures that are eaten on *smørrebrød* or as an appetiser. *Italiensk salat* consists of diced carrots, asparagus, peas and macaroni. *Skinkesalat* is basically chopped ham, while *sildesalat* comprises marinated or pickled herring, beetroot and apple. These are only the most common of the many sandwich salads generally available.

Skål! ...and tak!

Learn to say *skål* (the vowel is between 'loll' and 'hall') with your beer or *akvavit*. It's more than just Danish for 'cheers', it's a ritual if you are invited to a Danish home. Your host usually has the privilege of making the first toast, and will raise a glass, point it towards everyone in turn, looking directly at them, and say '*skål!*'. After all have taken a sip or a swallow, the host will look at each again in turn before putting down the glass.

After the meal itself, the appropriate – and essential – words to say are '*tak for mad*' (pronounced 'tak for maad'), meaning, very simply, 'thanks for the meal'.

Cheese and Fruit

Danish Blue *(Danablue)*, a rich, sharp-flavoured cheese, has always had a strong international following. Mycella is fairly similar in taste, but is milder. Fynbo and Samsø, both relatively mild and firm cheeses, possess a sweet, almost nutty flavour.

Desserts

It will have been obvious from the time you arrived that Denmark is not a good place for dieting. And by the time you get to the desserts your best intentions will have been quite definitely routed. Your dessert will almost certainly be laced with cream *(fløde)* or whipped cream *(flødeskum)*.

People-watching is part of the experience at Copenhagen's outdoor eateries.

Favourite desserts include: *æblekage* (stewed apples with vanilla, served with alternating layers of biscuit crumbs and topped with whipped cream) and *bondepige med slør* (a mixture of rye-bread crumbs, stewed apple, sugar and the ubiquitous whipped cream).

Snacks

For a snack with a difference, try the deep-fried Camembert cheese served with toast and strawberry jam *(ristet franskbrø med friturestegt camembert og jordbærsyltetøj)*. The university area is good for cheap goulashes, hashes, chicken and *håndmadder* (usually three slender *smørrebrød* with different toppings). Hot-dog stands *(pølsevogn)* are found everywhere, serving red Danish sausages *(pølse)* with mustards and relishes.

Curiously, Danish pastry is known here as Viennese pastry *(wienerbrød)*. This distinctive light and flaky delight can be found in any konditori, and makes a delectable snack in the middle of the morning or afternoon.

Drinks

Golden Danish lager comes in several types: *lys pilsner* (light lager) which has only 2 percent alcohol; the more normal green-bottle pilsner; and the stouts and special beers (such as Carlsberg Elephant) at 6 to 7 percent or more. Pilsner is available everywhere almost 24-hours a day. In cafés it costs three or four times the shop price. Draught beer *(fadøl)* is less fizzy and slightly cheaper.

Akvavit is fiery Danish schnapps made from potatoes, often with a caraway taste. The colour varies according to the herbs

Beer: Bottles and Cans

Beer, *øl* (draught beer is known as *fadøl*), can be expensive in Denmark, but it is much cheaper when purchased from a shop. Supermarkets and other stores are open until 5.30pm on weekdays and 2pm on Saturday, although some smaller shops do stay open until 8 or 9pm during the week, but they will charge you more for the privilege. Technically, it is illegal to sell beer outside these hours and on Sunday and public holidays, though some of the smaller shops turn a blind eye to the law. There is a deposit for each bottle, which may be refunded at any store.

***The assortment of drinks is endless in Copenhagen. But if
you want to sample a local spirit, try the** akvavit.*

and spices that have been used for flavouring. It is sipped at
mealtimes during the opening fish course or with the cheese,
and will sometimes be washed down with a beer chaser. If you
order *akvavit* with your meal, the bottle may occasionally be
put on the table for you to help yourself. Don't be deluded into
thinking you'll only be charged for a single measure – back in
the bar they'll know exactly how much has gone.

All wines are imported and while there is a wide selection
of French, German and Italian varieties, they are always
rather expensive in restaurants. Even cheap house wine
(*husets vin*) may be three times the supermarket price. After
your dinner, try the Danish cherry liqueur, *Cherry Heering*.

Coffee (*kaffe*) can be found everywhere – rich, strong, and
served with cream. The price may seem high, but the waiter
will usually come around offering refills. On a chilly day you
might like to try *varm kakao med flødeskum* – a hot cocoa
with whipped cream.

To Help You Order …

Could we have a table?		**Kan vi få et bord?**	
Do you have a set menu?		**Har De en fast menu?**	
I'd like a/an/some …		**Jeg vil gerne have …**	
beer	en øl	napkin	en serviet
bread	brød	pepper	peber
coffee	kaffe	potatoes	kartofler
dessert	en dessert	salad	en salat
fish	fisk	salt	salt
glass	et glas	soup	suppe
ice cream	is	sugar	sukker
meat	kød	tea	te
menu	et spisekort	vegetables	grønsager
milk	mælk	(iced) water	(is) vand
mustard	sennep	wine	vin

…and Read the Menu

agurkesalat	cucumber salad	**kål**	cabbage
blomkål	cauliflower	**lagkage**	layer cake
citron	lemon	**lever**	liver
flæskesteg	roast pork and crackling	**løg**	onion
		medisterpølse	pork sausage
grøn peber	green pepper	**nyre**	kidney
grønne bønner	French beans	**oksekød**	beef
gulerødder	carrots	**pommes frites**	French fries
hamburgerryg	loin of pork	**porre**	leek
hindbær	raspberry	**rødkål**	red cabbage
jordbær	strawberry	**svinekød**	pork
kartoffelmos	mashed potatoes	**søtunge**	sole
kirsebær	cherry	**æble**	apple
kotelet	chop	**æg**	egg
kylling	chicken	**æggekage**	omelette

HANDY TRAVEL TIPS

An A–Z Summary of Practical Information

A

ACCOMMODATION *(hotel; indlogering)* (See also CAMPING, YOUTH HOSTELS, and the list of RECOMMENDED HOTELS starting on page 126)

Since 1997 all hotels that are members of the Association of the Hotel, Restaurant, and Tourism Industry in Denmark (HORESTA) have been classified on a scale of one to five stars, based on objective criteria. Rates on page 126 are averages for double rooms in high season, service charges and taxes included, but these can be down by as much as 50 percent at other times of the year. You will find that a hearty Danish breakfast is usually included in the rate.

A Hotel Guide is available from any Danish Tourist Board office.

The Copenhagen Tourist Information, Bernstorffsgade 1; tel: 70 22 24 42; fax: 70 22 24 52; e-mail <touristinfo@woco.dk> is located directly across from the central railway station, open 9am–8pm in the summer months, and can assist you with accommodation either before you leave home, or upon arrival in Copenhagen.

AIRPORT *(lufthavn)*

Copenhagen Airport, Kastrup, <www.cph.dk>, around 10km (6 miles) from the city centre, is considered to be the main northern European hub, and is one of the continent's busiest airports.

The quickest way to Copenhagen city centre – Central Station – is on the fast train link that leaves from track 2 (located under Terminal 3) three times every hour, takes just 12 minutes and costs 25kr each way.

The airport bus runs from the airport every 15 minutes, takes 25 minutes to Central Station and costs 35kr.

The regular bus, 250S, departs from outside Terminal 3 every 15 minutes between 5.30am–midnight, takes 35 minutes, and costs 16.50kr.

Taxis take between 20–30 minutes, expect to pay 120–160kr.

Where's the bus for ...?   **Hvorfra afgår bussen til ...?**

B

BICYCLE RENTAL *(cykeludlejning)*

The City Bike Foundation, Brøstes Gård, 8 Overgaden Oven Vandet, tel: 32 54 00 79; fax: 32 54 01 39; web site <www.bycyklen.dk>, has 2,500 free city bikes at racks throughout the city centre. Simply take one out by putting 20kr into the slot. Remember, though, you can only use it within the limits shown – you are subject to a 1,000kr fine if stopped by police outside City Bike Country – and when you return it to a City Bike rack you get your 20kr back.

Much better to rent a decent bike from one of the many bike shops. This costs about 70kr per day for a three-speeder. Bikes can be put on S-tog trains except during rush hours. Look for carriages with a cycle symbol.

BUDGETING FOR YOUR TRIP

The following are some average prices in Danish kroner (kr) for basic expenses. However, remember that all prices must be regarded as approximate. Danes round off the bill, up or down, to the closest amount possible divisible by 25 øre because there are no intermediate coins (eg, 13 is rounded off to 25).

Airport transfer. Bus to Rådhuspladsen 16.50kr. Special airport bus directly to Central Station 35kr; taxi 140kr.

Camping. Camping pass for foreign visitors 30kr per person per night, children half price.

Car rental. Ford Focus 1.6 approx. 800kr per day, 3,500kr per week; Volvo V70 (station wagon) 1,400kr per day, 5,500kr per week; Opel Vectra (automatic) 1,100kr per day, 4,800kr per week; all prices include unlimited mileage, insurance, and local taxes.

Copenhagen Card. One day City card cost 159kr; three-day Plus Card cost 395kr *(see page 124)*.

Travel Tips

Entertainment. Cinema 60–80kr, Royal Ballet tickets 70–400kr, nightclub entry 60–100kr. Tivoli Gardens: adults 60kr, children half price.

Hotels. 5-star 2,500kr; 4-star 1,600kr; 3-star 1,200kr; 2-star 800kr; 1-star 600kr. These are average rack rates for the year 2002, and include breakfast, VAT and service.

Meals and drinks (at a fairly good establishment). Lunch 100kr, dinner 150/250kr, sandwich *(smørrebrød)* 20–30kr, coffee 15kr, *akvavit* (schnaaps) 30kr, beer 40kr, soft drink 25kr.

Public transport. Flat-rate ticket *(grundbillet)* for single bus or S-train ride 14kr. Ticket coupons *(rabatkort)* for 10 rides: blue 90kr, yellow 120kr, brown 165kr, lilac 200kr, orange 240kr, grey (all zones) 230kr.

Shopping bag. Bread 16kr, 250g of butter 12kr, 6 eggs 10kr, ½ kg of beefsteak (choice meat) 75kr, 200g of instant coffee 45kr, bottle of beer 6kr, soft drink 5kr.

Taxi. The basic fare is 23kr *(see page 121)*.

CAMPING

There are more than 500 approved camping sites in Denmark for tents, caravans and campers. Several also have cabins for rent. These are inspected annually and classified with a one- to five-star rating. All the 2- to 5-star sites have facilities for motor homes. You must obtain a Camping Pass valid for one calendar year and these are available at any camping site office for 80kr for an individual, or for a couple or a family (comprising children under 18 years old). A pass for a single overnight stay costs 20kr. No camping is permitted outside official sites.

You can pick up a comprehensive free brochure on camping, youth hostels and student hotels from the Danish Tourist Board in your country *(see page 124)*. Alternatively, for general information on camping in Denmark and sites in and around Copenhagen, contact Campingrådet, Mosedalsvej 15, 2500 Valby; tel: 39 27 88 44; fax 38 27 80 44; <www.campingraadet.dk>.

CAR HIRE *(biludlejning)* (See also DRIVING and BUDGETING FOR YOUR TRIP)

In reality, visitors to Copenhagen and the numerous attractions in its immediate vicinity will find that having a car is more of a hindrance than an assistance, especially because the public transport system is superb. Car rental, like fuel, is not inexpensive and traffic offences such as drink-driving have incredibly severe penalties.

If you decide to rent once you are in Copenhagen, then contact Avis, tel: 33 26 80 00, <www.avis.dk>; Europcar, tel: 33 55 99 00, <www.europecar.dk>; Hertz, tel: 33 17 90 20, <www.hertzdk.dk>; or Budget, tel: 33 55 70 00, <www.budget.dk>

To rent a car, you will need a valid national (or international) driver's licence and be at least 20 years of age (25 for some companies). Most agencies will require payment by credit card.

CLIMATE and CLOTHING

Climate. Denmark's relatively temperate climate is due to its situation and the sea currents, but frequent switches in the wind also bring changeable weather. Spring may come late, but summer is often sunny and autumn mild. Average monthly temperatures in Copenhagen are:

	J	F	M	A	M	J	J	A	S	O	N	D
°C	0.5	0	2	6	11	16	17	16	13	9	5	2
°F	33	32	35	42	52	60	63	61	56	48	40	36

Clothing. Casual clothes will be suitable for nearly every occasion, including the theatre and most dining out. Only in top-class hotels, restaurants and clubs – and even then not uniformly – will men be required to wear a tie in the evening, and here women will not look out of place in something dressy. Otherwise, go as you like. Summer nights are long and light but often chilly, so a sweater or cardigan is essential. Bring a light overcoat or raincoat, too, in addition to ordinary summer clothes – the weather has an awkward habit of changing. On the beach, you can be as undressed as you like.

Spring and autumn have many hours of sunshine, but winter can be downright cold and you should pack plenty of warm clothes (plus a raincoat). In all seasons, comfortable walking shoes are highly recommended for your excursions on foot around town.

COMPLAINTS

The Danish sense of fair play makes complaining a rare event, and complaints themselves often unnecessary. In a restaurant or hotel, a quiet word with the manager is usually enough. Serious complaints about hotels or other services should be directed to the Copenhagen tourist offices (see page 123) or to the appropriate travel authority.

CRIME (See also EMERGENCIES and POLICE)

Copenhagen is no longer among the safest capital cities in Europe. Pickpockets are rampant and petty crime is on the increase. Take normal precautions. Keep a close eye on your belongings. Hesitate before walking out alone in the very early hours through seedy areas – your hotel receptionist can give advice if you are in doubt about night-time locations that you wish to visit. It is also best to be very careful in the Christiania area, both by day and night.

It is a good policy to place your valuables – including passport and airline tickets – in the hotel safe. Another sensible precaution is to take photocopies of passports and airline tickets and keep them separate from the originals. In instances where the originals are stolen, lost or damaged, this will save an enormous amount of time and hassle.

Any loss or theft should be reported at once to the nearest police station, if only for insurance purposes; your insurance company will need to see a copy of the police report.

CUSTOMS and ENTRY FORMALITIES *(tull)*

Visitors from Britain and most countries outside the EU need a valid passport to enter Denmark; citizens from EU countries, excluding Britain, need only an identity card. You are generally entitled to stay in Denmark for up to three months without a visa (this period includes the total amount of time spent in Denmark, Finland, Iceland, Norway and Sweden in any six-month period.)

South African citizens will need a visa. Contact the Embassy of Denmark, Senlam Centre, 8th Floor, Pretorius/Andries Streets, Pretoria, 0002, South Africa, tel: (27) 012 322 0595; fax: (27) 012 322 0596. European and North American residents are not subject to any health requirements. In case of doubt, check with Danish representatives in your own country before departure.

Duty-free allowance. As Denmark is part of the European Union, free exchange of non-duty-free goods for personal use is permitted between Denmark and other EU countries. Due to the high prices of alcohol and tobacco visitors might consider bringing in some of their own. If so, each person over 20 is allowed 1 litre of liquor (over 22 percent by volume) and 200 cigarettes (or 50 cigars) if living in the EU, and 400 cigarettes if living outside the EU.

DRIVING

If you take your car into Denmark from the UK then you will need a valid driver's licence, car registration papers, a Green Card (an extension of your regular insurance policy, valid for travel abroad – though not obligatory for EU countries, it's still preferable to have it), a red warning triangle in case of breakdown and a national identity sticker for your car. British car-owners note: left dipping headlights are illegal.

Travel Tips

Driving conditions. Drive on the right, pass on the left. Traditionally, traffic coming from your right has priority, and clear indication should always be given when changing lanes. Weaving from one lane to another is a punishable offence.

Pedestrian crossings are sacrosanct and nearly always controlled by lights. Beware of buses pulling out from stops – you should give way to them. Use caution for cyclists and moped riders to your right, often on their own raised paths *(cykelsti)*, but sometimes divided from you merely by a white line, which you should not cross.

Seat belts must be worn by driver and passengers. Motorcycle, moped and scooter drivers, and their passengers, must wear helmets.

Speed limits. On the *motorvej* (motorway), the limit is 110km/h (68mph). On other roads it is 80km/h (50mph) and in built-up areas – indicated by white signs with town silhouettes – it drops to 50km/h (30mph). Cars with caravans may not exceed 70km/h (44mph). If you are caught speeding, there's a heavy, on-the-spot fine.

Drinking and driving. The penalties are severe: If you are discovered to have more than 0.5 milligrams per thousand litres of alcohol in your blood while driving, you face severe penalties

Road signs. International pictographs are in widespread use in Copenhagen, but below are translations of some local signs:

Blind vej	Dead-end road (cul-de-sac)
Fare	Danger
Fodgængere	Pedestrians
Indkørsel forbudt	No entry
Omkørsel	Diversion
Rabatten er blød	Soft shoulders
Udkørsel	Exit
Vejarbejde	Roadworks

Fluid measures

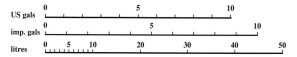

Distance

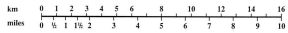

ELECTRICITY

The supply for electric appliances in Denmark is 220 volt, 50 Hz AC, and requires standard two-pin, round continental plugs. Visitors should bring their own adapters.

EMBASSIES/CONSULATES

The embassies, with consulate sections, are generally open Mon–Fri 8am–4pm, but there is usually a 24-hour telephone service. New Zealand does not have an embassy in Denmark.

Australia: embassy: Dampfærgevej 26, 2nd floor, DK-2100 Copenhagen Ø; tel/fax: 70 26 36 76; consulate: Strandboulevarden 122, DK-2100 Copenhagen Ø; tel: 39 29 20 77.

Canada: embassy: Kristen Bernikowsgade 1, DK-1105 Copenhagen K; tel: 33 48 32 00; fax: 33 48 32 20.

Republic of Ireland: embassy: Østbanegade 21, DK-2100 Copenhagen Ø; tel: 35 42 32 33; fax: 35 43 18 58.

South Africa: consulate: Gammel Vartovvej 8, DK-2900 Hellerup; tel: 39 18 01 55; fax: 39 18 40 06

UK: embassy and consulate: Kastelsvej 40, DK-2100 Copenhagen Ø; tel: 35 44 52 00; fax: 35 44 52 53.

Travel Tips

USA: embassy and consulate: Dag Hammarskjölds Allé 24, DK-2100 Copenhagen Ø; tel: 35 55 31 44.

EMERGENCIES (see also POLICE and MEDICAL CARE)
The all-purpose emergency number is 112 and is free from public phone boxes. Ask for police, fire or ambulance. Speak distinctly (English will be understood) and state your number and location.

For medical emergencies, doctors are on call Mon–Fri 8am–4pm (tel: 33 93 63 00). During other hours tel: 38 88 60 41.

Dental emergency. Tandlægevagten, Oslo Plads 14, is open Mon–Fri 8am–9.30pm; Sat–Sun and public holidays 10am–noon; tel: 35 38 02 51. Cash payment only.

GAY and LESBIAN TRAVELLERS

Denmark has one of Europe's most liberal attitudes towards gays and lesbians, and this is reflected in its legislation. In common with most of Scandinavia, the age of consent is the same as for heterosexuals. Copenhagen has a thriving gay scene, and there are bars, clubs and a few hotels where gays are openly welcome. For information, contact the Landsforeningen for Bøsser og Lesbiske (National Association for Gays and Lesbians), Teglgårdstræde 13; tel: 33 13 19 48; <www.lbl.dk.>

GETTING TO COPENHAGEN

Air Travel

From the UK: The following airlines are among those operating regular services to Copenhagen: SAS (Scandinavian Airlines System; tel: 0845 607 2772; <www.scandinavian.net>), Maersk Air (tel: 020 7333 0066; <www.maersk-air.com>), British Airways (tel: 0845 773 3377; <www.britishairways.com>), British Midland (tel: 0870

6070 555; <www.flybmi.com>), EasyJet (tel: 0870 600000; <www.easyjet.com>), Virgin Express (tel: 0800 891 1999; <www.virginexpress.com>).

From the USA & Canada: SAS (Scandinavian Airlines System), tel: 1-800-221-2350; <www.flysas.com>, operates daily flights to Copenhagen from Newark and Chicago.

From Australia and New Zealand: There are no direct flights from these countries. Depending upon the city of destination Qantas, the Australian national airline, operates in conjunction with other airlines. Flights to Copenhagen necessitate two, sometimes three, changes, usually in the Far East and then Europe. Air New Zealand operates flights from Auckland to London and then from London on BA to Copenhagen.

Rail Travel

You can travel to Copenhagen by train from London Liverpool Street to Harwich, then by DFDS Seaways to Esbjerg and onwards by train to Copenhagen (tel: 08707 333 000). Alternatively, you can take Eurostar from London Waterloo International to Brussels and a connecting service to Copenhagen (Rail Europe, tel: 0870 584 8848).

Rail Passes. Rail Europe, tel: 0870 584 8848; <www.raileurope.co.uk>, offers a variety of rail passes that must be purchased before leaving home, and can be used in Denmark alone or in Denmark and other Scandinavian and/or European countries.

Coach Travel

Contact Eurolines (tel: 0870 514 3219; <www.eurolines.co.uk>) for details of coach services from London to Copenhagen.

GUIDES and TOURS *(guide)*

The Association of Authorised Guides offers individual and group tours. For reservations tel: 33 11 33 19, fax: 33 11 37 05, <www.guides.dk>. Open Tues and Thurs 12.30pm–3.30pm.

Travel Tips

Canal and harbour tours. DFDS Canal tours (tel: 33 42 33 20; <www.canal-tours.dk>) and Netto Boats (tel: 32 54 41 02; <www.netto-baadene.dk>) run 50-minute guided canal tours from Apr–Oct between 10am and 5pm (7pm in July and Aug). The DFDS tours depart from Nyhavnand Gammel Strand; Netto tours depart from Holmens Church. DFDS also run 'hop-on-hop-off' canal tours from 10am–5pm. The unbroken voyage lasts 90 minutes. Kayak Tours (tel: 40 50 40 06; <www.kajakole .dk>) depart from Gammel Strand for 1½–3hr canal voyages in kayaks equipped with intercom.

Brewery visits. A brewery tour is an excellent way to spend time, not only to sample a free bottle or two, but also to discover how every glass you drink is a contribution to art, science or industry: Carlsberg and Tuborg donate vast sums through their charitable foundations. Carlsberg (tel: 33 27 13 14; fax: 33 27 47 09; <www.carlsberg.com>) is near the famous Elephant Gate, Gamle Carlsbergvej 11 (bus 6 from Rådhuspladsen); tours Tues–Sun 10am–4pm.

City tours. Copenhagen Excursions (tel: 32 54 06 06; <www.cex.dk>) and Auto Paaske/Vikingbus (tel: 32 66 00 00; <www.sightseeing.dk>) depart from in front of the Palace Hotel at Rådhuspladsen (City Hall Square) every 30 minutes from Apr–Oct on 'hop-on-hop-off' city tours. The same companies run Grand Tours lasting 2½ hours. These depart throughout the year at 11am with additional departures daily mid-May–Sept at 1.30pm and Oct–mid-May Sat 1.30pm. These companies also run City & Harbour Tours, which last 2½ hours and depart from mid-May–Sept 9.30am, 11.30am, 1pm and 3pm.

Copenhagen's cycle culture has extended to the introduction of trishaws. Three companies run city tours and taxi services using trishaws. The basic city tour fare is 75kr; when used as taxis the flag-drop is usually 25kr. Haggling is not inappropriate. Quickshaw Bike Taxis (tel: 70 20 13 75; <www. quickshaw. bix>), Rickshaws (tel:

35 43 01 22; <www.rickshaw.dk>), Cykeltaxi (tel: 70 26 00 55; <www.cykeltaxi. com>) uses motor-assisted pedal power.

Industrial art tours. Guided tours in English of the Royal Copenhagen porcelain factory, Smallegade 45, tel: 38 14 92 97, Mon–Fri 9am–3pm. Similar tours are available for silver and glass works.

Trips to Sweden. Sweden is so close and accessible that it really is worth the short trip – if only to see how Swedes differ from Danes. Trains to Malmö over the Øresund Bridge take 35 minutes. An alternative is to combine a trip to Helsingør with the 20-minute ferry service to Helsingborg in Sweden. The more adventurous can try a 'Round the Sound' trip. Buy tickets from DSB (Danish State Railways; tel: 70 13 14 15; <www.dsb.dk>) and travel to Malmö, then to Helsingborg by train, across the sound to Helsingør, and back to Copenhagen by train.

H

HEALTH & MEDICAL CARE

Make sure your health insurance covers any illness or accident while travelling. Your travel agent or insurance company will advise you.

In Denmark, treatment and even hospitalisation is free for any tourist taken suddenly ill or involved in an accident. For minor treatments, doctors, dentists and pharmacists will charge on the spot. For EU members, this money will be partly refunded at the local Danish health service office on production of receipts and the form E111, obtainable from post offices in the UK.

A Danish pharmacy *(apotek)* is strictly a dispensary. Pharmacies are listed in the phone book under *Apoteker*. Opening hours are 9am–5.30pm and until 1pm on Sat An all-night service operates at Steno Apotek, Vesterbrogade 69, tel: 33 14 82 66; and at Sønderbro Apotek, Amangerbrog 158, tel: 32 58 01 40.

Travel Tips

I need a doctor/dentist. **Jeg har brug for en læge/tandlæge.**

HOLIDAYS *(fest-/helligdag)*

Though Denmark's banks, offices and major shops close on public holidays, museums, cafés and tourist attractions will be open.

1 January	Nytår	New Year's Day
5 June (half-day)	Grundslovsdag	Constitution Day
24/25/26 December	Christmas	
31 December	New Year's Eve	

Movable dates:

Skærtorsdag	Maundy Thursday
Langfredag	Good Friday
Anden påskedag	Easter Monday
Bededag	General Prayer Day (fourth Friday after Easter)
Kristi himmelfartsdag	Ascension Day
Anden pinsedag	Whit Monday

L

LANGUAGE

English is widely spoken and understood. Danish is perhaps the most difficult northern-European language for relating the written word to speech; it's almost impossible to pronounce simply by reading the words, as many syllables are swallowed rather than spoken. Thus the island of Amager becomes Am-air, with the 'g' disappearing, but in a distinctively Danish way difficult for the visitor to imitate. The letter 'd' becomes something like a 'th', but with the tongue placed behind the lower teeth, not the upper. The letter 'ø' is like the 'u' in English 'nurse', but spoken with the lips far forward. And the letter 'r' is again swallowed.

There are 29 letters in the Danish alphabet including 'æ' (as in egg), 'ø', and 'å' (as in port). They appear after the usual 26 (a point to note when looking up names in phone books and lists).

Days

Monday	mandag	Friday	fredag
Tuesday	tirsdag	Saturday	lørdag
Wednesday	onsdag	Sunday	søndag
Thursday	torsdag		

Months

January	januar	March	marts
February	februar	April	april
May	maj	September	september
June	juni	October	oktober
July	juli	November	november
August	august	December	december

Numbers

0	nul	10	ti	20	tyve
1	en	11	elleve	30	tredive
2	to	12	tolv	40	fyrre
3	tre	13	tretten	50	halvtreds
4	fire	14	fjorten	60	tres
5	fem	15	femten	70	halvfjerds
6	seks	16	seksten	80	firs
7	syv	17	sytten	90	halvfems
8	otte	18	atten	100	hundrede
9	ni	19	nitten	1000	tusind

LAUNDRY and DRY CLEANING *(vask; kemisk rensning)*
The large hotels offer same-day service, but generally not at weekends and holidays – and it's usually expensive. Dry cleaners are found throughout the city and are listed in the phone book *(Fagbog)*

under *Renserier*. Prices in launderettes *(selvbetjeningsvaskeri)* are lower, and these are open until late at night.

When will it be ready?	**Hvornår er det færdigt?**
I must have this for tomorrow morning.	**Jeg skal bruge det i morgen tidlig.**

LOST PROPERTY *(hittegods)*
The general lost-property office *(hittegodskontor)* is at the police station at Slotsherrensvej 113, Vanløse (tel: 38 74 52 61), Mon, Wed, Fri 9am–2pm, Tues and Thurs 9am–5.30pm. For property lost in buses or trains contact Lyshøjgårdsvej 80, Valby; tel: 36 13 14 15, open daily 7am–9.30pm. For missing credit cards: American Express, tel: 80 01 00 21; Diners Club, tel: 36 73 73 73; Access, Eurocard, Eurocheques, MasterCard, JCB and Visa, tel: 44 89 25 00. All operate a 24-hour service.

M

MEDIA

Newspapers and magazines *(avis; ugeblad)*. You'll have no problem finding English-language newspapers and magazines at newsstands, shops and hotels throughout central Copenhagen. The kiosk at the Central Station sells foreign-language publications, and there is a good selection at Magasin du Nord (Kongens Nytorv13) and Illums (Østergade 52-54) department stores. There is also a free monthly English-language booklet, *Copenhagen This Week*, which lists comprehensive information for visitors.

Radio and TV *(radio; fjernsyn)*. There is a news programme in English on Radio Station P3 (93.8 MHz) at 8.30am Mon–Fri. BBC long-wave and world services and European-based American networks can be picked up. Most hotels have satellite TV with stations from the USA and UK.

Have you any English-language newspapers?	**Har De engelsksprogede aviser?**

MONEY MATTERS

Currency. The unit of Danish currency is the kroner, abbreviated kr, or, abroad, DKK (to distinguish it from the Norwegian and Swedish kroner). It is divided into 100 øre.

Coins: 25 and 50 øre; 1, 2, 5, 10 and 20 kroner.
Banknotes: 50, 100, 200, 500 and 1,000 kroner.

Banks and currency-exchange offices *(bank; vekselkontor).* Banks and exchange bureaux offer the best exchange rates for foreign cash. You pay a flat commission per transaction at banks, which are open Mon–Fri 9.30am–4pm (until 6pm Thurs), although some at airports and the main railway stations keep longer hours. Outside banking hours, exchange bureaux operate at the Central Station, the airport and other locations.

Credit cards and travellers cheques *(kreditkort; rejsecheck).* Most institutions these days will accept payment by most international credit cards. Credit/debit cards can also be used in ATM machines to obtain kroner (cheaper and more convenient than exchanging cash). Travellers cheques can be cashed at banks, provided you bring along your passport.

Tax. Danish VAT (sales tax) is called MOMS and is set at 25 percent. It's always included in the bill. For purchases totalling a minimum of 300kr in any one store, foreign visitors can claim a tax refund. Look for shops displaying the Global Tax-Free Shopping sign; retailers are well-acquainted with the necessary procedures.

OPENING HOURS

Banks are open Mon–Fri 9:30am–4pm, Thurs until 6pm. In the provinces, hours fluctuate from town to town.

Post offices are open 9 or 10am–5 or 5.30pm during the week; some post offices are also open on Sat 9am–1pm.

Shops and department stores are generally open Mon–Fri 9am or 10am–5.30pm or 7pm; recently Danish shopping hours have been officially extended, permitting shops to be open from 6am to 8pm if they wish. Some are closed on Monday or Tuesday. Shops are usually open from 9am–1 or 2pm on Saturday. Some shops in Copenhagen, especially in the tourist areas, stay open for longer hours.

Museums are often closed on Monday and generally open for shorter hours during the winter.

POLICE (See also Emergencies)

State and city police all form part of the national force and are dressed in black uniforms. Some walk their beat through central Copenhagen, but most policemen patrol in dark-blue-and-white or white cars with the word *'politi'* in large letters. You are entitled to stop police cars at any time and request help. Police are courteous and speak English.

Don't hesitate to go to the local police station if in need of advice.

Where's the nearest police station?	**Hvor er den nærmeste politi-station?**

POST OFFICES *(postkontor)*

The main post office is at Tietgensgade 35–39 (just behind Tivoli); business hours are Mon–Fri 11am–6pm, Sat 10am–1pm. The post office at the Central Station operates longer hours: Mon–Fri

8am–10pm, Sat 9am–4pm, Sun 10am–5pm. There are also many sub-offices around town. All post offices display a red sign with a crown, bugle and crossed arrows in yellow – and a sign saying *Kongelig Post og Telegraf*. When buying postcards from stands and souvenir shops, you can get the appropriate stamps on the spot. Danish letterboxes are bright red and stand out cheerfully, as do the postmen – colourful characters in red uniforms riding yellow cycles. You can pick up poste restante mail at the main post office at Tietgensgade 35–39 (postal address: DK-1500 Copenhagen V); identification is necessary.

PUBLIC TRANSPORT

HT Buses and S-Train. An excellent public transport system with frequent bus and electrified train (S-tog) service covers not only Copenhagen, but its extensive metropolitan area. For HUR information, tel: 36 13 14 15 (7am–9.30pm), or consult <www.hur.dk>; for S-train information see <www.dsb.dk>.

Metro. (tel: 70 15 16 15; <www.orestadsselskabet.dk>) Fully automated trains cover parts of the city on two lines – M1 and M2. They run at frequent intervals between 5am and 1am with special night services on Friday and Saturday.

Tickets. The Copenhagen metropolitan area is split into seven zones and a ticket allows travel on buses, S-trains and the metro. A basic ticket permits travel within two zones for one hour and costs 15kr (7kr for children). Two-zone tickets cover most places mentioned in this book. A 24-hour ticket costs 85kr (children 42.50kr) and permits 24 hours of unlimited travel. Discount clip cards *(klippekort)* are available for 10 journeys. A two-zone card costs 95kr (children 45kr). The duration of the validity of tickets and discount clip cards depends on the numbers of zones in which you travel: 2–3 zones – 1 hour; 4–6 zones – 1½ hours; all zones – 2 hours.

Travel Tips

Harbour Bus. (www.ht.dk) This travels six times an hour from 6am–6pm between the Royal Library on Christians Brygge and the Little Mermaid with stops at Nyhaven and Holmen North.

Taxis. Plenty of taxis cruise the streets of Copenhagen, but in wet weather it can be difficult to find a vacant one. They are recognisable by a Taxi or *Taxa* sign, and vacant cabs display the word *fri* (free). Tipping is not necessary, but round the sum up if you are impressed by the service. The basic fare is 23kr plus 10kr per km between 6am–4pm, 11kr 4pm–6am, 13kr Fri–Sat 11pm–7am and on Sunday and national holidays. Most drivers accept credit cards.

Trains *(tog)*. A comprehensive and punctual network, which covers the entire country, operates from Copenhagen Central Station.

R

RELIGION

The Danish Church is Protestant (Danish Lutheran Evangelical), and 92 percent of the Danes are members.

Sunday services in English are held in these places of worship:

Church of England. St Alban's Anglican Episcopalian Church, Churchillparken, Langelinie. Sunday morning services, Holy Communion 9am and Family Eucharist 10.30am; Wednesday Holy Communion 10.30am (tel: 39 62 77 36).

Roman Catholic. Sacrament's Church (Sakrementskirken), Nørrebrogade 27. Services in English Sunday 6pm and Wednesday 5pm. (tel: 44 94 76 78).

Jewish services. Great Synagogue, Krystalgade 12. Friday at sundown and Saturday at 9pm (tel: 33 12 88 68).

Mormons. Latter Day Saints, Nitivej 63. Sunday at 10am (tel: 38 34 10 21).

T

TELEPHONES *(telefon)*

The country code for Denmark is 45 and the city code for Copenhagen is 33. The country code for Great Britain is 44, the USA and Canada 1, Australia 61, New Zealand 64, the Republic of Ireland 353 and South Africa 27.

Phone boxes generally take prepaid telephone cards that can be purchased from shops and kiosks. Remember, calls from your hotel room are always expensive.

TIME ZONES

Denmark operates on Central European Time (GMT + 1). In summer, the clock is put one hour ahead (GMT + 2), and the time differences look like this:

New York	London	**Copenhagen**	Jo'burg	Sydney
7am	noon	**1pm**	1pm	9pm

What time is it, please?   **Undskyld, hvad er klokken?**

TIPPING

In general you don't give tips unless special services have been rendered. Hotel and restaurant bills always include service. Railway porters charge fixed prices, and there is no need to tip hairdressers, or taxi drivers. You may like to leave the odd kroner tip for use of the washbasin and facilities in toilets.

TOILETS

Facilities are usually indicated by a pictograph; alternatively they are marked WC, *Toiletter, Damer/Herrer* (Ladies/Gentlemen), or just D/H. There is no charge unless you see it clearly marked otherwise.

TOURIST INFORMATION *(turistinformation)*

In Copenhagen the main place to go is the Copenhagen Tourist Information office, Bernstorffsgade 1, across from Central Station and

Travel Tips

just outside Tivoli (open May–Aug Mon–Sat 9am–8pm, Sun 10am–8pm; Sept–Apr Mon–Sat 9am–4pm; tel: 70 22 24 42; fax 70 22 24 52; e-mail <touristinfo@woco.dk>). Besides offering a comprehensive array of tourist information, posters and postcards, the office also offers personal assistance with booking sightseeing tours and hotel and private accommodation.

Copenhagen Card. The Tourist Information office is also one of the many places where you may purchase the Copenhagen Card. The City Card lasts for one day and gives free or reduced admission to 40 popular museums and sights in the city. Cost is 159kr (children 10–15 years 90kr). The Plus Card is valid for 72 hours and gives free or reduced admission to 70 popular museums and sights in Greater Copenhagen. It also grants free travel on buses, S-trains, Metro and Waterbus throughout the region as well as discounts on car hire and Scandlines ferry routes between Denmark and Sweden. The cost is 395kr (children 10–15 years 225kr). With these cards two children under 10 years may accompany each adult free of charge.

All Danish cities and most small towns have their own tourist information office marked by a large letter 'i' on a green background.

UK: Danish Tourist Board, 55 Sloane Street, London SW1X 9SY; tel: 020 7259 5959; fax 020 7259 5955; e-mail <dtb.london@dt.dk>.

US: Danish Tourist Board, 655 Third Avenue, 18th floor, New York, NY 10017; tel: (212) 885-9700; fax (212) 885-9726.

Where's the tourist office?   **Hvor ligger turistbureauet?**

WEBSITES

The Danish Tourist Board has comprehensive information at <www.visitdenmark.com>, and Wonderful Copenhagen has a wealth of information at <www.woco.dk>. Other websites are listed alongside the individual entries throughout Travel Tips.

WEIGHTS and MEASURES

For fluid and distance measurements, *see page 111*. Denmark uses the metric system.

Length

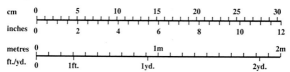

| cm | 0 | | 5 | | 10 | | 15 | | 20 | | 25 | | 30 |
| inches | 0 | | 2 | | 4 | | 6 | | 8 | | 10 | | 12 |

| metres | 0 | | | | 1m | | | | | 2m |
| ft./yd. | 0 | 1ft. | | | 1yd. | | | | 2yd. | |

Weight

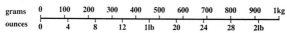

| grams | 0 | 100 | 200 | 300 | 400 | 500 | 600 | 700 | 800 | 900 | 1kg |
| ounces | 0 | 4 | 8 | 12 | 1lb | 20 | 24 | 28 | 2lb | | |

Temperature

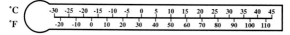

| °C | -30 | -25 | -20 | -15 | -10 | -5 | 0 | 5 | 10 | 15 | 20 | 25 | 30 | 35 | 40 | 45 |
| °F | -20 | -10 | 0 | 10 | 20 | 30 | 40 | 50 | 60 | 70 | 80 | 90 | 100 | 110 | | |

Y

YOUTH HOSTELS *(vandrerhjem)*

There are 10 city youth hostels and student hotels. Youth hostels require a membership card issued by an organisation affiliated to the International Youth Hostel Association. If you haven't got such a card, you can obtain a guest card from Danmarks Vandrerhjem (Denmark's Youth Hostels), Vesterbrogade 39, DK-1620 Copenhagen V; tel: 31 31 36 12; fax 31 31 36 26; <www.danhostel.dk>. Open Mon–Thurs 9am–4pm, Fri until 3pm. During Apr–Aug Thurs 9am–6pm

At a student hotel *(ungdomsherberg)*, restrictions on night-time closing and other practices are more relaxed.

Recommended Hotels

Most of Copenhagen's hotels tend to be clustered near Central Station, within a very short walking distance of the city's main sights – Rådhuspladsen, the lively shopping area along Strøget and Tivoli Gardens.

The following Copenhagen establishments are listed alphabetically within their star rating, with price categories based on the cost per night of a double room with bath or shower (unless indicated otherwise) in the high season, including service charge, VAT (MOMS) and breakfast. These rates can be as much as 50 percent lower at other times of the year.

It is always advisable to reserve ahead of your stay. The city is at its busiest in the summer months (June–August), but conferences ensure that hotels are kept busy throughout the year.

€€€€	over 2,000kr
€€€	1,500–2,000kr
€€	1,000–1,500kr
€	under 1,000kr

Hotel d'Angleterre (5 stars) €€€€ *Kongens Nytorv 34, DK-1058 Copenhagen K; tel: 33 12 00 95; fax: 33 12 11 18; <www.remmen.dk>*. Established more than 250 years ago, this is Copenhagen's finest and grandest hotel. With a superb location overlooking Kongens Nytorv, it has been named the Best Hotel in Denmark for several years running. 124 rooms.

Marriott (5 stars) €€€ *Kalvebod Brygge, 1560 Copenhagen V; tel: 88 33 99 00; www.marriott.com/cphdk*. A luxury glass and concrete block offers all that one expects from Marriott hotels. Waterside rooms offer splendid views over the inner harbour. 395 rooms.

Radisson SAS Royal (5 stars) €€€€ *Hammerichsgade 1, DK-1611 Copenhagen V; tel: 33 42 60 00; fax: 33 42 61 00; <www.radissonsas.com>.* Dating from 1960, this modern 20-storey, centrally located hotel offers a panoramic view of Tivoli Gardens and city. Rooms in modern Danish design, rooftop restaurant, sauna and private parking. 265 rooms.

Skt Petri (5 stars) €€€€ *Krystalgade 22, DK-1172 Copenhagen K; tel: 33 78 87 61; <www.hotelsktpetri.com>.* This brilliant conversion of a renowned department store situated in the Latin Quarter is Copenhagen's newest hotel. Scandinavian chic at its best; Bang & Olufsen televisions. 27 suites. 270 rooms.

Copenhagen Admiral Hotel (4 stars) €€ *Tolbodgade 24-28, DK-1253 Copenhagen K; tel: 33 74 14 14; fax: 33 74 14 16; <www.admiral-hotel.dk>.* Standing beside the harbour, the hotel was formerly a granary constructed in 1787. Comfortably converted, it has retained the 200-year-old Pomeranian pine wooden beams in the rooms. Features its own restaurant, night club and sauna. 366 rooms.

First Hotel Vesterbro (4 stars) €€€ *Vesterbrogade 23-29, DK-1620 Copenhagen V; tel: 33 78 80 00; fax: 33 78 80 80; <www.firsthotels.com>.* Opened in 1999, it was the third largest in Denmark and the first newly built hotel in Copenhagen for more than 15 years. Modern rooms, excellent service and just a five-minute walk from Tivoli and Rådhuspladsen. 403 rooms.

Grand Hotel (4 stars) €€€ *Vesterbrogade 9A, DK-1620 Copenhagen V; tel: 33 31 36 00; fax: 33 31 33 50;*

Recommended Hotels

<www.grandhotelcopenhagen.dk>. An enticing façade, dating from 1890, fronts a hotel that has been carefully modernised in a manner that preserves much of its original character. Tastefully decorated rooms; ask for a corner one. 161 rooms.

Hotel Kong Arthur (4 stars) €€€ *Nørre Søgade 11, DK-1370 Copenhagen V; tel: 33 11 12 12; fax: 33 32 61 30; <www.kongarthur.dk>*. Inaugurated in 1882, and situated beside Peblinge Lake, this hotel has retained much of its original charm. A popular choice with both Danish and foreign visitors; it has a friendly and thoroughly Danish atmosphere. 107 rooms.

Hotel Kong Frederik (4 stars) €€ *Vester Voldgade 25, DK-1552 Copenhagen V; tel: 33 12 59 02; fax: 33 93 59 01; <www.remmen.dk>*. Although named in 1898, its history as hotel and inn dates back to the 14th century. Very close to Rådhuspladsen and Tivoli, a recent renovation retained its classical English ambience. 110 rooms.

Imperial Hotel (4 stars) €€€–€€€€ *Vester Farimagsgade 9, DK-1606 Copenhagen V; tel: 33 12 80 00; fax: 33 93 80 31; <www.imperialhotel.dk>*. With a good location next door to Vesterport Station and a few minutes' walk from Rådhuspladsen, this is a splendid hotel. Modern, well-appointed rooms, fine restaurants and on-site parking. 163 rooms.

Phoenix Copenhagen (4 stars) €€€ *Bredgade 37, DK-1260 Copenhagen K; tel: 33 95 95 00; fax: 33 33 98 33; <www.phoenixcopenhagen.dk>*. An elegant deluxe hotel close to the Royal Palace and Kongens Nytorv. All rooms and suites are air-conditioned and furnished elegantly in the French Louis XVI style. 213 rooms.

Recommended Hotels

Palace Hotel (4 stars) €€€ *Rådhuspladsen 57, DK-1550 Copenhagen V; tel: 33 14 40 50; fax: 33 14 52 79; <www.palace-hotel.dk>.* An imposing historical landmark on Rådhuspladsen, the Palace has been carefully renovated and modernised over the years to the highest standards. Forty Ambassador Class rooms overlook Rådhuspladsen and Tivoli Gardens. 162 rooms.

Radisson Falconer Hotel (4 stars) €€€ *Falkoner Allé 9, DK-2000 Frederiksberg; tel: 38 19 80 01; fax: 38 87 11 91; <www.radissonsas.com>.* In a pleasant location near Copenhagen Zoo and just 2km (1 mile) from the city centre. Tropical atrium lobby and rooms in either Scandinavian, Oriental or Art Deco styles. 166 rooms.

Radisson Scandinavia Hotel (4 stars) €€€ *Amager Boulevard 70, DK-2300 Copenhagen S; tel: 33 96 50 00; fax: 33 96 55 00; <www.radissonsas.com>.* A 25-storey building that dominates the skyline just outside the city centre. Rooms furnished in Standard, Scandinavian or Oriental décor, with most having fine views. Casino, fitness centre, pool. 542 rooms.

Scandic Hotel Copenhagen (4 stars) €€€ *Vester Søgade 6, DK-1601 Copenhagen V; tel: 33 14 35 35; fax: 33 32 12 23; <www.scandic-hotels.com>.* Modern, 18-storey building offering a whole range of facilities, including restaurants, cafés, bars, a health club and on-site parking. 472 rooms.

Sofitel Plaza Hotel (4 stars) €€€ *Bernstorffsgade 4, DK-1577 Copenhagen V; tel: 33 14 92 62; fax: 33 93 93 62; <www.accorhotel.dk>.* Commissioned by Frederik VIII in 1913, this hotel has beautifully appointed rooms and lovely decoration throughout. The attractive Library Bar has been

Recommended Hotels

voted one of the five best bars in the world by *Forbes Magazine*. 93 rooms.

Sophie Amalie Hotel (4 stars) €€ *Sankt Annæ Plads 21, DK-1250 Copenhagen K; tel: 33 13 34 00; fax: 33 11 77 07; <www.remmen.dk>*. Named after the popular 17th-century queen, this hotel is located on the harbourfront adjacent to Amalienborg Palace and close to Nyhavn. Refurbished in 1986, it has comfortable, well-equipped rooms. 134 rooms.

71 Nyhavn Hotel (4 stars) €€€ *Nyhavn 71, DK-1051 Copenhagen K; tel: 33 11 85 85, 33 93 15 85; <www.71nyhavnhotelcopenhagen.dk>*. Delightfully located at the foot of Nyhavn in a well-renovated and carefully restored warehouse. A modern hotel with rather small rooms, a rustic ambience and great views over the harbour. 84 rooms.

Ascot Hotel (3 stars) €€ *Studiestræde 61, DK-1554 Copenhagen V; tel: 33 12 60 00; fax: 33 14 60 40; <www.ascothotel.dk>*. Set in a distinguished old building a few steps from City Hall, this hotel is pleasantly decorated with a mixture of antiques and modern furniture. 155 rooms.

City (3 stars) €€ *Peder Skramsgade 24, DK-1054 Copenhagen K; tel: 33 13 06 66; fax: 33 13 06 67; <www.hotel city.dk>*. Located in an elegant townhouse, the City has an international feel, clearly expressed in the hotel's striking modern décor. It has a hospitable and friendly ambience. 81 rooms.

Copenhagen Crown Hotel (3 stars) € *Vesterbrogade 41, DK-1620 Copenhagen V; tel: 33 21 21 66; fax: 33 21 00 66; <www.accorhotel.dk>*. At an address with more than 100 years of tradition, the entrance is in a quiet courtyard just off this busy street. Pleasant rooms, and just a few minutes' walk from Rådhuspladsen. 78 rooms.

Copenhagen Strand (3 stars) €€ *Havnegade 37, DK-1058 Copenhagen K; tel: 33 48 99 00; fax: 33 48 99 01; <www.copenhagenstrand.dk>.* Opened in 2000 this ultra-modern hotel is in a converted warehouse dating from 1869. On a side street just off Nyhavn, close to Kongens Nytorv. 174 rooms.

DGI-Byens (3 stars) €€ *Tietgensgade 65, 1704 Copenhagen V; tel: 33 29 80 50; <www.dgi-byen.dk>.* Situated very close to Central Station and Tivoli, this new hotel is Danish minimalism at its best. Some rooms with balconies. Conference facilities. Attached to the hotel is the Vandkulturhuset, Copenhagen's state-of-the-art swimming complex and spa. 104 rooms.

Hotel Alexandra (3 stars) €€ *H.C. Andersens Boulevard 8, DK-1553 Copenhagen V; tel: 33 74 44 44; fax: 33 74 44 88; <www.hotel-alexandra.dk>.* A lovely old hotel in a building originating from 1880, situated almost next door to Rådhuspladsen. Pleasantly decorated, with light, airy rooms and excellent facilities. 61 rooms.

Hotel Astoria (3 stars) €€ *Banegårdspladsen 4, DK-1570 Copenhagen V; tel: 33 14 14 19; fax: 33 14 08 02; <www.astoriahotelcopenhagen.dk>.* Dating from 1936, its bizarre façade is an excellent architectural example of Cubist style. The rooms have been updated to meet modern tastes; some have as many as five beds and are particularly suitable for families. 94 rooms.

Hotel Christian IV (3 stars) €€ *Dronningens Tværgade 45, DK 1302 Copenhagen K; tel: 33 32 10 44; fax: 33 32 07 06;*

Recommended Hotels

<www.christianivhotelcopenhagen.dk>. A small pleasing hotel located right by the lovely King's Garden. Rooms are neat and bright, and fitted with modern Danish furniture. 42 rooms.

Hotel Danmark (3 stars) €€ *Vester Voldgade 89, DK-1552 Copenhagen V; tel: 33 11 48 06; fax: 33 14 36 30, <www.hotel denmark.dk>*. Adjacent to Rådhuspladsen and close to Strøget. Modern bright building with rooms tastefully furnished in subdued Scandinavian style. Underground parking. 51 rooms.

Hotel Esplanaden (3 stars) €–€€ *Bredgade 78, DK-1260 Copenhagen K; tel: 33 48 10 00; fax: 33 48 10 66.* Located between Amalienborg and the Little Mermaid in the 250-year old Frederiksstad quarter. A newly renovated economy hotel, part of the Choice chain, with clean pleasant rooms. 117 rooms.

Hotel Opera (3 stars) €€ *Todenskjoldsgade 15, DK-1055 Copenhagen K; tel: 33 12 15 19; fax: 33 32 12 82; <www.operahotelcopenhagen.dk>*. Located close to the Royal Theatre at Kongens Nytorv. Dating from 1869, a recent renovation introduced 'Olde England' décor. 91 rooms.

IBIS Copenhagen Star (3 stars) € *Colbjørnsensgade 13, DK-1652 Copenhagen V; tel: 33 22 11 00; fax: 33 21 21 86; <www.accorhotel.dk>*. Another hotel in the cluster of streets on the other side of Central Station from Tivoli. Well-appointed rooms and an inviting Jacuzzi. 134 rooms.

IBIS Copenhagen Triton (3 stars) € *Helgolandsgade 7-11, DK-1653 Copenhagen V; tel: 33 31 32 66; fax: 33 31 69 70; <www.accorhotel.dk>*. In a building dating from the turn of the 20th century, this hotel is located two blocks from Central Station. Two categories of rooms and non-smoking rooms. 123 rooms.

Ibsens Hotel (3 stars) €€ *Vendersgade 23, DK-1363 Copenhagen K; tel: 33 13 19 13; fax: 33 13 19 16; <www.ibsenshotel.dk>*. Located between Nørreport Station and Peblinge Lake, in a pleasant area about a 15-minute walk from the city centre. A comfortable small hotel, recently renovated. 101 rooms.

Mayfair Hotel (3 stars) €€ *Helgolandsgade 3, DK-1653 Copenhagen V; tel: 33 31 48 01; fax: 33 23 96 86; <www.themayfairhotel.dk>*. An early 20th-century hotel that has recently been refurbished. It offers a cosy atmosphere coupled with a very high standard of personal service. 106 rooms.

Mercure Hotel Copenhagen (3 stars) € *Vester Farimagsgade 17, DK-1606 Copenhagen V; tel: 33 12 57 11; fax: 33 12 57 17; <www.accorhotel.dk>*. Just behind Vesterport Station, this is a pleasant tourist class hotel, with an outdoor tennis court available to guests for a small fee. 109 rooms.

Mercure Hotel Richmond Copenhagen (3 stars) €€ *Vester Farimagsgade 33, DK-1780 Copenhagen V; tel: 33 12 33 66; fax: 33 12 97 17; <www.accorhotel.dk>*. Also close to Vesterport Station, this is slightly more upmarket than its sister hotel, the Copenhagen. Sound-proof windows. 127 rooms.

The Square (3 stars) €€€ *Rådhuspladsen 14, DK-1550, Copenhagen V; Tel: 33 38 12 00; <www.thesquare.dk>*. In the heart of Rådhuspladsen this new air-conditioned hotel is the conversion of an office block. Several grades of rooms. Rooftop breakfast room with fine views. 192 rooms (46 singles).

Centrum (2 stars) € *Helgolandsgade14, 1653 Copenhagen D; tel: 33 31 31 11; <www.hotelcentrum.dk>*. Newly refurbished hotel close to Central Station. Functional bedrooms.

Recommended Restaurants

With more than 2,000 restaurants, cafés, bars and snack bars, many of them serving ethnic cuisine, Copenhagen is something of a gourmet's paradise. This particularly applies to the six establishments that were awarded Michelin stars in 2003. Whether you fancy a quick coffee and wienerbrød or a five-course feast, you'll have plenty of places to choose from. There are nearly 40 eating establishments alone inside Tivoli Gardens, while the nearby Scala Centre has numerous bars and restaurants. For lunch, cafés serve a selection of hot dishes and smørrebrød (open sandwiches) at reasonable prices. Dinner can be as light or as heavy as you like, and many places offer traditional Scandinavian smörgåsbord (open table), where you can eat as much as you like for a set charge.

The establishments below are a cross-section of what is available. Prices are based on the cost of a meal for two people, including tax but excluding drinks. Note that the high import duty on wine can add considerably to the final bill. For an up-to-date listing of eating establishments, consult the free monthly *Copenhagen This Week* (see page 118).

€€€€€	over 1,000kr
€€€€	between 500–1,000kr
€€€	between 250–500kr
€€	between 100–250kr
€	below 100kr

Restaurationen €€€€€ *Møntergade 19, DK-1116 Copenhagen K; tel: 33 14 94 95.* A charismatic restaurant, very much reflecting the owners', Bo & Lisbeth Jacobsen, personalities. One fixed menu using only seasonal produce, changed weekly, that costs 1,000kr per person and is explained at your table by Bo – using a board and easel. Open Tuesday–Saturday for dinner, closed July.

Era Ora €€€€–€€€€€ *Torvegade 62, Christianshavn, Copenhagen; tel: 32 54 06 93; fax: 32 96 02 09; <www.era-ora.dk>.* Opened in 1983, this restaurant offers Italian cuisine presented innovatively. The most expensive of the three set menus features antipasti, pasta, meat or fish, cheese and then a dessert. One Michelin star. Open Monday–Saturday for dinner.

Kommandanten €€€€–€€€€€ *Ny Adelgade 7, DK-1104 Copenhagen K; tel: 33 12 09 90; fax: 33 93 12 23; <www.kommandanten.com>.* In a 1698 town house and decorated by the floral artist and interior designer, Tage Andersen, this 2-star Michelin restaurant, the only one in Denmark, is both a visual and culinary experience. Open Monday–Friday lunch and dinner, Saturday dinner.

Kong Hans Kælder €€€€–€€€€€ *Vingaardsstræde 6, DK-1070 Copenhagen K; tel: 33 11 68 68; fax: 33 32 67 68; <www.konghans.dk>.* Located in the oldest building in Copenhagen, whose Gothic arches give it a medieval ambience. It has its own salmon smokehouse, classical French cuisine, and very fine wines. One Michelin star. Open Monday–Saturday, dinner.

Krogs Fiskerestaurant €€€€–€€€€€ *Gammel Strand 38, DK-1202 Copenhagen K; tel: 33 15 89 15; fax: 33 15 83 19; <www.krogs.com>.* In an 18th-century building with early-20th-century décor, this restaurant is justly renowned for its excellent fish dishes. Reservations are strongly recommended. Kitchen open Monday–Saturday from 11.30am–midnight.

Recommended Restaurants

Den Gyldne Fortun €€€€ *Ved Stranden 18, DK-1061 Copenhagen K; tel: 33 12 20 11; fax: 33 93 35 11; <www.den-gyldne-fortun.dk>.* An established fish and shellfish restaurant situated across the canal from Christiansborg. Three-, four- and five-course menus. Open Monday–Saturday 11.30am–midnight, Sunday between May and September 11.30am–midnight, and at other times 5.30pm–midnight.

Egoisten €€€€ *Hovedvagtsgade 2, DK-1103 Copenhagen K; tel: 33 12 79 71; fax: 33 91 63 19; <www.egoisten.dk>.* Classic French food and a Danish lunch, carefully prepared and pleasingly presented. Open Monday–Saturday 11.30am–3.30pm and 5.30–10.30pm, closed Sunday.

Konrad €€€€ *Pilestræd 12-14, 1112 Copenhagen K; tel: 33 93 29 29; <www.restaurantkonrad.dk>.* The 'in' place in Copenhagen. Well-presented and beautifully prepared French/Scandinavian food. A DJ plays from 11pm onwards on Thursday, Friday and Saturday. Open Monday–Wednesday noon–midnight; Thursday till 1am, Friday–Saturday till 3.30am.

Pierre André Fransk Restaurant €€€€ *Ny Østergade 21, DK-1101 Copenhagen K; tel: 33 16 17 19.* Opened in early 1996 and gained a Michelin star after just one year. A 35-seat dining room decorated in terracotta, the cuisine is modern French/Italian classic with the menu changing every two months, and an exclusive wine list. Open Monday–Saturday for dinner.

Restaurant Godt €€€€ *Gothersgade 38, DK-1123 Copenhagen K; tel: 33 15 21 22. Godt* means good; an under-statement for this small, family-run 20-seat restaurant. The cuisine is European with one daily four-course menu, a mainly

French, although expanding, wine list. One Michelin star and reservations required. Open Monday–Saturday for dinner.

Els €€€–€€€€ *Store Strandstræde 3, DK-1255 Copenhagen K; tel: 33 14 13 41; fax: 33 91 07 00; <www.restaurant els.dk>.* The elegant 19th-century décor of this delightful restaurant close to Kongens Nytorv complements the stylish cuisine. Fish is a speciality, and the menu changes every day. Reservations are strongly advised. Open daily for lunch and dinner.

Lumskebugten €€€–€€€€ *Esplanaden 21, DK-1263 Copenhagen K; tel: 33 15 60 29.* A small and exclusive restaurant by Churchill Park near the Little Mermaid statue. Fine food, fine wine. It is also runs the Royal Barge moored nearby. Reservations are essential. Open Monday–Friday for lunch and dinner, Saturday dinner.

Restaurant Balkonen Tivoli €€€–€€€€ *Vesterbrogade 3, DK-1620 Copenhagen V; tel: 33 11 27 85; <www.balkonen. dk>.* Located on a prominent balcony overlooking a Tivoli Gardens. Varied menu with seafood, a carvery and a popular salad bar. Open daily for lunch and dinner.

Restaurant L'Alsace €€€–€€€€ *Ny Østergade/ Pistolstræde; tel: 33 14 57 43; fax: 33 12 80 21; <www.alsace.dk>.* Situated in a charming courtyard surrounded by 17th-century buildings. An interesting and diverse menu, with specialities such as Iberian ham, oysters, caviar and other seafood. Open Monday–Saturday for lunch and dinner.

A Hereford Beefstouw €€€ *Tivoli, Vesterbrogade 3, DK-1620 Copenhagen V; tel: 33 12 74 41.* Juicy steaks cooked to order and tasty seafood dishes. A restaurant chain with a difference; a percentage of the profits are invested in quality art that adorns the restaurants. Open daily for lunch and dinner.

Café à Porta €€€ *Kongens Nytorv 17, DK-1050 Copenhagen K; tel: 33 11 05 00; fax: 33 11 05 52; <www. cafe aporta.dk>*. One of the city's oldest and most popular cafés, dating from 1788. Ideal stop for a meal or a drink. Café open all day, restaurant from 5.30pm–10.30pm.

Café Ketchup €€€ *Pilestræde 19, 1112 Copenhagen K; Tel; 33 32 30 30; <www.cafeketchup.dk>*. Inventive fusion cuisine – Asian, Danish, French – served in a modern café at the front or in the restaurant behind and below. DJ on Friday and Saturday. Open Monday–Wednesday 11am–midnight, Thursday till 1am, Friday and Saturday till 3am. Also in Tivoli, *tel: 33 75 07 55*.

Café Ultimo €€€ *Tivoli, Vesterbrogade 33, 1630 Copenhagen V; tel: 33 75 07 51; <www.cafeultimo tivoli.dk>*. Inspired Italian cuisine served in what was once a dance hall, then a hippodrome. Open daily noon–10pm. Also at *Hovedvagtsgade 8, tel: 33 33 99 97; <www.cafeultimo.dk>*.

Copenhagen Corner €€€ *Rådhuspladsen, Vesterbrogade 1A, DK-1620 Copenhagen V; tel: 33 91 45 45; fax: 33 91 04 04; <www.remmen.dk>*. Excellent French/Danish cuisine in a brightly decorated restaurant overlooking City Hall. Open daily from 11:30am until midnight.

Fyrskibet €€€ *Nyhavn 61, 1051 Copenhagen K; tel: 33 11 19 33; <www.fyrskibet.com>*. Dine aboard a lighthouse ship berthed at the foot of Nyhavn. Drinks and snacks on the deck; meals in a glass enclosed cabin. Fish a speciality. Open Monday–Saturday 10.30am–11pm.

Le Sommelier €€€ *Bredgade 63-65, DK-1260 Copenhagen K; tel: 33 11 45 15, 33 11 59 79; <www.lesommelier.dk>.* French in name and French in style, with a large bar and dining area. Forty wines by the glass and, reputedly, the largest cellar in Denmark. Open Monday–Friday for lunch and dinner, Saturday and Sunday for dinner.

Passagens Spisehus €€€ *Vesterbrogade 42 1620, Copenhagen V; tel: 3 22 47 57; <www.passagens.dk>.* The place for Nordic food. Starters include dried cod and Lapland carpaccio; main courses feature wild musk from Greenland, reindeer and moose. Affordable set meals in somewhat stark décor. Good wines. Open Tuesday–Thursday 6pm–10pm, Friday and Saturday 5pm–11pm.

Restaurant Gråbrødre Torv 21 €€€ *Gråbrødretorv 21, DK-1154 Copenhagen K; tel: 33 11 47 07; fax: 33 12 60 19; <www.graabrodre21.aok.dk>.* Whether in the charming dining rooms or outside in this pleasant square, eating here is a delight. Danish specialities well-prepared and presented. Special set-price 'quick-lunch'. Open daily for lunch and dinner.

St Gertruds Kloster €€€ *Hauser Plads 32, DK-1127 Copenhagen K; tel: 33 14 66 30; fax: 33 93 93 65; <www.skt-gertrud.dk>.* The vault of a 14th-century monastery is the setting for this restaurant offering specialities from around the world and a wine cellar of more 39,000 bottles. Reservations advised. Open daily from 5pm–11pm.

Restaurant Bali €€–€€€ *Lille Kongensgade 4, DK-1074 Copenhagen K; tel: 33 11 08 08.* Located on the corner of Kongens Nytorv, this restaurant has a tropical ambience. Indonesian cuisine, including *rijstaffel* and a selection of lovely,

Recommended Restaurants

delicately spiced meat and vegetable dishes. Open daily noon–midnight.

Carlton €€ *Halmtorvet 14, 1700 Copenhagen V; tel: 33 29 90 90;* *<www.carltonkbhu.dk>*. Trendy new restaurant and café in located in an up-and-coming area. Delightful ambience, limited menu, great outdoor space. Vegetarian brunch is served till 3pm. Open Monday–Friday 10am–midnight, Saturday–Sunday till 2am.

India Palace €€ *H.C. Andersens Boulevard 13, DK-1553 Copenhagen V; tel: 33 91 04 08*. This place serves authentic Indian cuisine in pleasant surroundings just a short step from Rådhuspladsen. The restaurant's delicious all-you-can-eat lunch and dinner buffet provide excellent value. Open daily 11am–midnight.

Københavner Caféen €€ *Badstuestræde 10, DK-1209 Copenhagen K; tel: 33 32 80 81*. A delightful restaurant just off Strøget, particularly recommended for its Danish cold table and the daily *Copenhagen Plate* offering seven items for a very reasonable set price. Open daily noon–10.30pm.

Mongolian Barbecue €€ *Stormgade 35, Copenhagen; tel: 33 14 63 20*. This popular restaurant provides an excellent-value Mongolian buffet with as much as you can eat for a set price. Open daily 4pm–midnight.

Nyhavns Færgekro €€ *Nyhavn 5, DK-1051 Copenhagen K; tel: 33 15 15 88; fax: 33 15 18 68;* *<www.nyhavns faergekro. dk>*. An unpretentious restaurant serving particularly good traditional food. It's renowned for its herring buffet. Wonderful location alongside Nyhavn; sit inside or outside. Open daily 11.30am–11.30 pm.

Rio Bravo €€ *Vester Voldgade 86, DK-1552 Copenhagen V; tel: 33 11 75 87.* No-nonsense cowboy-style steak house, where even the seats at the bar are saddles. A popular restaurant and a firm favourite with late-night revellers. Open Monday–Saturday 12.30pm–4am, Sunday from 5pm.

Café Sommersko €–€€ *Kronprinsessegade 6, DK-1114 Copenhagen; tel: 33 14 81 89; <www.sommersko.dk>.* Just off Strøget, this is a lively Danish/French café. Varied menu; numerous foreign beers. Kitchen open Monday–Friday 8am–10pm, Saturday 9am–10pm, Sunday 10am–10pm.

Govindas Vegetar Restaurant €–€€ *Nørre Farimagsgade 82, DK-1364 Copenhagen K; tel: 33 33 74 44; <www.govindas.aok.dk>.* A small unpretentious vegetarian restaurant close to the Botanisk Have. Open Monday–Friday noon–8.30pm.

Slotskælderen has Gitte Kik €–€€ *Fortunstræde 4, 1065 Copenhagen K; tel: 33 11 15 37.* Come here for delightful *smørrebrød* served in a cosy basement. Open Monday–Saturday 10am–5pm.

Ankara € *Krystalgade 8-10, 1172 Copenhagen K; tel: 33 15 19 15; <www.Ankara.dk>.* Extensive Turkish buffet modified to suit the Danish palate. Inexpensive wines and coffees. A belly dancer provides entertainment. Open Monday–Saturday 1pm–midnight, Sunday 2pm–midnight.

RizRaz € *Store Kannikstræde, 1169 Copenhagen D; 19 tel: 33 32 33 45; <www.rizraz.dk>.* RizRaz does a splendid Mediterranean vegetarian buffet; however, meat dishes may also be ordered and are served at table. Open daily 11am–midnight. Also at *Kompagnistræde 20, 1208 Copenhagen K; tel: 33 15 05 75.*

INDEX